CONNECTED

FOCUSING ON 'ME' AND 'WE'

RACHEL JOHNSON

Together we unlock every learner's unique potential

At Hachette Learning (formerly Hodder Education), there's one thing we're certain about. No two students learn the same way. That's why our approach to teaching begins by recognising the needs of individuals first.

Our mission is to allow every learner to fulfil their unique potential by empowering those who teach them. From our expert teaching and learning resources to our digital educational tools that make learning easier and more accessible for all, we provide solutions designed to maximise the impact of learning for every teacher, parent and student.

Aligned to our parent company, Hachette Livre, founded in 1826, we pride ourselves on being a learning solutions provider with a global footprint.

www.hachettelearning.com

To order, please visit www.HachetteLearning.com or contact Customer Service at education@hachette.co.uk / +44 (0)1235 827827.

ISBN: 978 1 0360 0729 4

© Rachel Johnson 2026

First published in 2026 by
Hachette Learning (a trading division of Hodder & Stoughton Limited),
An Hachette UK Company
Carmelite House
50 Victoria Embankment
London EC4Y 0DZ
www.HachetteLearning.com

The authorised representative in the EEA is Hachette Ireland, 8 Castlecourt Centre, Dublin 15, D15 XTP3, Ireland (email: info@hbgi.ie)

Impression number   10 9 8 7 6 5 4 3 2 1
Year   2030 2029 2028 2027 2026

Illustrations by DC Graphic Design Ltd.
Typeset in the UK.
Printed in the UK.

A catalogue record for this title is available from the British Library.

MIX
Paper | Supporting responsible forestry
FSC™ C104740

To all the young people I have had the pleasure to work with in the past and in the present. I hope that this book helps you have a more connected future.

About the author

Rachel Johnson is an author, podcaster, keynote speaker and the CEO of PiXL. A former teacher, now business leader, Rachel's work focuses on the things that get us stuck whether that is in the classroom or the boardroom, in our lives or in our leadership, as children or as the CEO. Her books for adults include *Time to Think: The Things that Stop Us and How To Deal With Them*; *Time to Think 2: The Things That Stop our Teams and What To Do About Them*; and *Box Clever: Quadrants To Change the Way We Live and Lead*. Rachel writes and hosts two podcasts: PiXL Pearls and the PiXL Leadership Bookclub.

A passionate advocate for young people, *Connected: Focusing on 'Me' and 'We'* is Rachel's first book for this age group.

Acknowledgements

This book was in my head many years ago. I didn't do anything about it then, but I have often thought about it since then. Then I met some wonderful young people who told me the things that got them stuck and it reminded me of why I thought these issues were important. Those young people helped me shape this book, some without even realising it, both many years ago when I was teaching, and now. My thanks go to those young people and the many who I have met when visiting schools.

There are so many students from my past who shaped me, and ultimately this book, without ever even realising it, all of whom are well into adulthood now: Darren, Michael, Maimie, Lily, Alex, Roderick and Sherif.

In my present, I know some amazing young people: Charlotte, Daniel, Matthew, Ethan, Jessica, Kenzie, Lex, Anna, Zoe, Ben, Lou, Talia, Raya, Georgie and Pippa. Thanks too to the young people of Ovingham Middle School who were happy to be interviewed about a range of issues and whose insight was so helpful before I started writing. For generous amounts of time, feedback and comments, thanks to Nick Reed and the students at Reintegreat in Middlesbrough: Paulbarry, Rihan, Isaac, Amber, Ethan and Leo. The work that happens at Reintegreat is truly impressive and connected. Thanks to Scott Wilson, Jo Whetstone, Ben Robertson and Lisa Fox from Hayfield School and to their young people who reviewed this book and expressed themselves so brilliantly: Louise, Matthew, Toby, Sadie, Harriet, Dylan and Luke. Your willingness to invest in young people so that they can be their best is inspiring.

To you, the one reading this book, thank you. I want you always to remember that you are a limited edition. You have value and you have purpose. There is no one like you. You have more power than you may realise; use it for good and to do good. Make great choices for you that benefit you but also make great choices to help those around you. We are all connected and all our actions have consequences; let's make them positive ones.

The way to live a fulfilled, happy and healthy life is to connect more, not less. We are connected, and the better we can be at living together side by side, the better we will all be. That's the challenge of this book. Get connected and stay connected. You won't regret it.

Reviews

Young people

I feel like this book gave me a head start on understanding situations I am likely to face as I grow up.

Practical advice and strategies to help us deal with challenges properly.

Louisa Pidgeon, Year 8

The book was insightful and quite eye-opening. I found a lot of the concepts genuinely fascinating and made me think more deeply about things I hadn't really considered before.

A profoundly fascinating and enlightening read.

Matthew Stott, Year 10

So many times I found myself thinking, 'Wow, that's literally happened to me,' the ideas are so easy to apply to real life.

I now understand the value different people bring and the different perspectives they can offer. I think it has helped me grow emotionally and become a better person.

Toby Hamilton, Year 10

I liked how the book puts some of my thoughts and feelings into words.

Sadie Robertson, Year 9

I learned more about how to regulate my emotions and how to cope with growing up.

I was surprised by how much some of the topics in the book related to my own life and situations that I have found myself in.

Harriet Brown, Year 8

I liked how it spoke directly to me and simplified complicated topics and allowed me to understand the importance of human connection.

This book is essential.

Dylan Hartley, Year 10

This book gives very useful tips.

Luke Caldwell, Year 9

This book helps you cope with situations. It can help you understand how you are and get help as it is sometimes embarrassing to ask others.

Paulbarry Gardiner

I think a book like this can be helpful to teenagers who are struggling to have a relationship with their parents. When teens feel like their parents are constantly on their backs, having a go at them, this book might help if they read it together.

Rihan Connor

This book teaches you how to control your emotions.

Isaac Almond

I could use the ideas in this book when my emotions are too much.

Amber Stone

I think this book could help lots of people if they read it and understand why they get angry and manage their responses to situations.

Ethan Ambrose

I think that there are lots of strategies to help people in this book. It can help you to understand your emotions, how to deal with them and how to speak to other people.

Leo Thompson

Staff

The book provides accessible, non-patronising prompts and ideas that can open up meaningful conversations without feeling forced or overly formal.

Connected has the potential to make a powerful contribution to school culture by strengthening understanding, empathy and a sense of belonging across the whole community. By offering thoughtful, non-patronising guidance, the book supports young people in developing self-awareness, confidence and emotional literacy – all of which are foundational to positive behaviour, healthy relationships and engagement with learning.

School leaders, youth leaders and anyone working with young people will benefit greatly from reading it. The book is full of practical advice and thoughtful strategies that will help young people better understand themselves, their relationships, and where they fit in the world.

I'm truly grateful to Rachel for writing a book for young people that is so honest, supportive and empowering – and for doing so in such a respectful, non-patronising way.

Scott Wilson, Deputy Headteacher

This book creates a backbone to the ad hoc conversations which young people want and need to have as they grow into themselves. It brings the big questions and answers around relationships and big feelings into focus in a way I have not seen before.

What makes this book stand out is its honesty. It provides valuable learning for young people to understand themselves and the feelings that are often so hard to put into words. Imperfect moments can become seen as opportunities to grow and reflect, as well as understand themselves and their connections with others.

A reassuring, empowering read for young people and the adults who support them.

Jo Whetstone, Associate Assistant Headteacher: Alternative Provision

The sheer number of practicable ideas around communication and fostering healthy relationships makes *Connected* essential reading. The brilliant research-informed approach to laughter, gossip and glow-ups will really make teenagers think.

Connected celebrates the emotional nuances and ambiguity teenagers face, eschewing the often binary world they inhabit in favour of optimism, empathy and authenticity.

Ben Robertson, Assistant Headteacher

Contents

Introduction
Pleased to meet you

You might be wondering why I've written this book. You may also be wondering why you have been given it, or asked / told to read it (delete as appropriate!). If you have either of those 'wonderings' then let me answer both of those questions before we hit Chapter 1.

But first, a bit about me and then it will make sense as to why we are here, together on this literal page. I'm Rachel, I'm an author, podcaster, leadership coach and a CEO. I'm married to Paul, and we have three children.

For 13 years, I was a teacher in secondary schools and I loved it. I loved my subject (English) but I mainly loved working with young people. That's because I usually found them to be honest, funny and perceptive… they could create laughter, joy and a new perspective. During that time, it seemed to me that they were working out what mattered to them, what they wanted and what they planned to achieve. It felt like a pleasure to be alongside them for some of that. I learned a lot from them too. There were a few of them who said 'we can't wait to read your first book'. I thought they were joking, maybe they were, or maybe they saw in me what I couldn't see in myself at the time.

I also saw some of the struggles they faced. Growing up isn't always easy: not always knowing how to get emotions under control, sometimes making the wrong choices and then feeling stuck. Sometimes not knowing how to make things right again. I used to teach a lot of this through English literature when we talked about a character's motive and behaviour. But I didn't just want to talk about Macbeth and his wife, or Juliet and her husband – I wanted to talk with young people, about how to navigate some of these tricky things.

In 2013, I changed jobs and started working with the adults in some of your schools across the UK. And here's the surprising thing I learned: so many of the issues that we face in our teenage years are *not* just issues for teenagers. The adults I started to work alongside were finding themselves navigating a different version of a very similar thing. I, too, am working out some of these things.

Recently, I visited a school to speak to some young people aged 11 to 14 years old and, after chatting for a bit, I showed them the contents page of my book for adults. 'Are any of these topics relevant to you?' I asked them. 'Pretty much ALL OF THEM,' they replied. 'No one tells us how to do any of that.' And then they told me what they were struggling with, why and how.

That's when I saw it clearly. These were the same issues I saw when I was teaching, the same ones that I see in adults and now these young people were saying it too. We really are all connected. Different ages, experiences, abilities and family contexts. Yet whether you're 13 or 33, some of these issues are the same. At the end of my time with these young people, I told them, 'I'm going to write a book for you so we can talk about this'.

You're holding that book in your hands right now. The book my own students suspected I would write.

This is a book that talks about the things that no one else is talking about. A book that helps you navigate the way forward with practical steps. A book that helps you see that we are all connected, and the way we interact with each other is crucially important for us all.

So why should *you* read this? Well, because it will help you now when you're a teenager and it will help you when you're not. You might be reading it on your own or you might be reading it as a class, but if we can do some of the things in this book, our world will be a better place for us all.

I hope this book will help you be an even more brilliant version of yourself. As you navigate the (sometimes) choppy waters of growing up, I hope this book helps you make connections and feel connected. Maybe you can even share this book with a friend or talk about what's in it, connecting with others in the process.

We need to connect with the 'me' – how **I** think and feel. We also need to connect with the 'we' – how **we** connect with others. It is in doing both that we can live happier and more fulfilled lives as individuals and as a society. We just need to work out how!

Chapter 1
Connected

Do you want to feel less lonely, feel you belong, be healthier in mind and body, live for longer and help others do the same? Connection is the first step! Let's find out how.

Humans need to feel that we have a connection with others and that we belong somewhere. We find this in lots of different places:

- In our families
- With our friends
- With people who have the same likes or dislikes as us
- As part of a group (like a club, school, form group or class group)
- With a faith community
- With people who see the world the same way we do.

> **Have a think:** Who are the people in your life who you have a connection with? What connects you with them?

When we really belong, we are not trying to 'fit in' or bend who we are to be acceptable in a group. If we really feel we belong, we feel seen and heard. It doesn't mean we always agree on everything or that things are perfect, but it means that we have a connection. Sometimes we make that connection visible, like when we wear a uniform, a sports strip or a certain style of clothes. All these things say clearly 'we are part of something together' (which is why, despite what your feelings may be on it, school uniform is a great symbol of belonging!). But connection goes far deeper than just what we wear.

Face the facts

Connection is a superpower!

Researchers have been studying the importance of connection, and it turns out that having social ties (however we find them) can impact our physical health, our mental health and our outlook on life. Sounds too good to be true? Take a look at the facts!

FACT 1: In an experiment, people were shown a hill. People who were climbing with friends estimated the hill to be less steep than those who were climbing alone. So walking with friends can reduce the size of hills? Well, in our heads anyway! If your walk home from school involves a steep hill, next time take some friends with you and feel it shrink!

FACT 2: The biggest factor in whether someone can recover from illness is the community of people they have around them. Social connection can reduce inflammation, lower our risk of serious health problems and can even help us live longer! Connection like this also saves money as, if people are healthier, fewer of them will be in hospitals or need doctors. If we connect with others, we are helping them live longer (and helping ourselves live longer in the process too!).

FACT 3: The World Health Organization says that communities who feel connection are often safer and healthier. They are also more resilient when responding to disasters. We saw this in the Covid-19 pandemic, and we will see it again when tough things happen in our communities.

FACT 4: When people feel connected, they perform better in problem-solving tests, are more creative and enjoy a greater level of professional success!

So surely, it's win-win? This is good news! When we are connected, we feel better, we might live longer, we perform better and we are more likely to overcome obstacles. If this is the case, why is it so hard? Why are we not trying harder to be more connected to each other?

WHY?!

An epidemic of loneliness

The *Cambridge Dictionary* defines an *epidemic* as when there is 'the appearance of a particular disease in a large number of people at the same time'. The word is beginning to be applied to other things – not just physical diseases. Researchers now talk about an 'epidemic of obesity', for example, and very recently an 'epidemic of loneliness'.

Why is this happening?

Nobody wants to be lonely, so why are so many people feeling this way?

1. Some researchers in America in 2020 found that there were some main causes of loneliness: too much time on technology, not enough time with family, being overworked or tired and the country feeling too individualistic. Too much 'me, me, me' and not enough 'we, we, we'.

2. Social media doesn't help us feel as connected as we think, even though we look more connected than ever before. Lots of studies now show that social media usually doesn't create genuine connection; it can actually make us more scared of being rejected and feel lonelier, and also encourages us to compare ourselves to other people. That doesn't sound quite as fun as the adverts! Despite that, it is addictive but can make us feel a bit more anxious as a result.

3. 'The liking gap': This is a term I bet you have experienced! The liking gap is when we think the other person we are talking to doesn't like us as much as we like them. We assume that we have enjoyed their company more than they have enjoyed ours. Then we get all shy and run away and we both think this of each other. That stops connection happening when it could have.

Change your world

In each chapter, you will find a section called 'Change your world'. There is a 'me' section for what you can do, and a 'we' section for what you could do together with your friends, your class or your school.

I could have called this section 'Change the world' but that might feel a bit big for you wherever you are sitting reading this. So, let's start small with something we CAN do. Each of us can change something about OUR world and if we all did that, we could change THE world. So, let's start!

ME

- Try finding someone in your class who you don't normally speak to and try to find something that you have a connection about.

- Try having more real face-to-face conversations instead of online ones. When we can see people's facial expressions and hear their tone of voice, it can be so much easier (and less stressful!).

- Find a way of telling people that you enjoyed chatting to them or spending time with them. I know this may make you cringe, and you don't want it to be cheesy, but if you don't say something the other person may think you hate them! That is how our minds work, and we can help ourselves and others by using words.

WE

- Play 'get to know you' activities that help you connect with your classmates (there are examples at the back of this book). There will be connections you may never see unless you try!

- If you have been together as a class a while, try this! Sit in a circle. Each person writes their name at the top of an A4 sheet of paper. Pass your paper with your name on it to the left. You now have a new sheet of paper with someone else's name on it. Everyone starts writing something encouraging about the person whose name is on the top. You could thank them for something, or comment on something you have appreciated, or say what you have noticed about them. All of it is positive and you must all agree this at the start. After 30 seconds (write quickly!) pass the paper to the left again. Repeat until you have completed one for everyone. At the end, you should get your own sheet of paper back with lots of lovely comments from your classmates. If you ever feel lonely, take it out and have a read.

- In your community, where may people feel lonely? What could you do together to help? Write letters each month from your class to the care home? Create a makeshift choir and go and sing for them? Run a coffee morning and invite people along?

You might think these suggestions are not for you – fine, no problem, I'm not offended (we have a chapter on that later!). It is totally fine if we disagree... but what COULD you do instead? Be creative, think differently, invent something of your own and do that.

Chapter 2
Comparison-itus

Do you sometimes compare yourself to other people and then feel worse about yourself? If you do, you're not on your own. There is another epidemic on the go, and this one is called Comparison-itus!

I want you to think about the last time you, and the people who look after you, fell out over something that you didn't think was fair. I want you to read the list below and mentally count how many of them you recognise.

The screentime scream:

Carer: You're not having any more screentime today.

You: But that's not fair, no one else's parents limit their kid's screentime, all my other friends are on it all the time.

The bed-time blues:

Carer: You need to go to bed now, it's very late.

You: None of my other friends are told when they should go to bed, they are treated like adults, not like little kids!

The influencer trap:

Carer: You're not having one of those, you're paying for the branded label, and I have never even heard of it or them.

You: What?! Literally everyone I know has one and I am going to look stupid if I don't, no one is wearing that thing you have bought me. Pleeease. I need it.

In all these examples, the heart of the argument is 'because everyone else is!'. This is part of comparison-itus. I am not doubting that you want more screentime, a later night and the latest brand BUT sometimes we want these things more because we perceive everyone else has them. We then think that we are being left out. That grows into us thinking everyone else has it way better than us. Then we get dissatisfied and *mad, bad* or *sad*.

- When we choose *mad*, we may shout and scream. (Obviously, I'm sure you don't do this!)

- When we choose *bad*, we start saying hurtful things that we don't mean or we deliberately go against what has been said and deceitfully do it anyway.

- When we choose *sad*, we feel multiple emotions that can feel quite overwhelming. We might say we feel sad because that's the big overarching word, but we could be feeling any of the following emotions and be unable to verbalise it: frustrated, disappointed, anxious, humiliated, lonely and a whole host more.

Is this just you? No, it's not. It's all humans. Here are some facts on comparison-itus.

FACT 1: Research in the early 2010s showed that interacting with Facebook (which was the main social-media platform at the time) negatively affected how people felt. The more they used it, the more their positive mood slipped away. The more people scrolled, the more envious they felt. That is hundreds of millions of people feeling bad about themselves and unhappy after being on social media.

FACT 2: According to research, 75% of people use social media for advice on what to buy.

FACT 3: 76% of users intend to buy something based on seeing a social-media post. That is why businesses love influencers – they make them money because what they say, we do! People are making big money because we can be so easily influenced because of comparison-itus.

Comparison-itus can be a very destructive thing. But do you have it?!

Here is a quick symptom checker:

- I feel jealous when I see what other people have and feel bad that I don't have it.

- I focus on people's highlight reels and forget that this is often staged, manufactured and edited to make it look good.

- I compare myself to others and then feel sad that my life looks less exciting / happy / brilliant than other people's seem to look.

- I am easily influenced by what I see and hear on social media.

- I start getting negative thought patterns about myself when I see what other people have.

- I feel like I am not good enough when I compare myself to others.

> **Have a think:** If you had to give yourself a score between 1 and 10 for how badly you suffer with comparison-itus, what would you score yourself? (10 means 'I always compare myself to others negatively'.)

The former American President Theodore Roosevelt used to say, 'comparison is the thief of joy'. That seems like a good description considering everything you have just read.

Maybe you would assume having read all this that I am going to say, 'don't compare yourself to anyone else – it's a terrible thing to do'. Well, surprise! Nope, actually you're wrong. Some comparison is a **good** thing. The trick is to do the RIGHT kind of comparing.

- **Comparison can help us make sense of ourselves.** We look to others to work out how well we are doing, to form opinions and to change our behaviour. For example, let's imagine you get 68% in a test. Is that good or bad? Until you compare what you got to the rest of the class, you can't really know. If everyone else got above 90%, you might want to change something about what you are doing (maybe do some revision, complete your homework or ask the teacher to help you with the questions that are causing the issues). If yours was the highest mark, then you would come to a different conclusion and act differently. There is a context that needs to be considered.

- **Comparison can help us know where we can add something special.** In a sports team, if you are better at position X but your teammate is better in position Y, the comparison helps place you both in the strongest positions. You would know where to play only by comparing your performance. That is a good thing, if comparing your skills and talents means the whole team is better. (This happens *all the time* in professional sport – that's literally the job of the manager and coach. It also happens in businesses, who want the best people in the right jobs too.)

- **Comparison can bring perspective to our problems.** Studies show that, when people are facing a difficult problem and are asked to think about someone who is facing something far worse, it helps bring comfort and helps them feel more optimistic. So, yes, sometimes you may find homework difficult, annoying or inconvenient, but think of all the children in the world who are banned from having any education at all. You will know about Malala Yousafzai. When she was 15, she was shot in the head when she was defending the right for girls like her to have an education. She and her classmates would have done anything to have the chance to do homework. So next time you're moaning over yours, let that comparison pop into your head: it might help.

- **Comparison can inspire us to make a change.** If you are wanting to be a songwriter or singer and you're comparing yourself to Taylor Swift, then you're probably going to find that doesn't go so well. There's you, with your £10 pocket money, and her with her $1.6 billion (£1.2 billion). BUT if you say to yourself, 'Taylor Swift wrote songs at 13 – she knew what she wanted, she worked hard, she did the work and, as a result, she succeeded against the odds. I can have that work ethic too', then that IS a helpful comparison. It spurs you on to DO something! (If you are not a Swiftie, insert another name that doesn't make you roll your eyes, but you get the idea!)

Change your world

ME

- If you are at the age where you are allowed social media or games, then why not limit your time on it. If you are going to use it, be aware that what you are seeing is not always real. Be mindful of what your emotions are doing when you're on it and get off it when you start noticing those feelings.

- Train your brain to compare yourself in helpful ways that are not destructive. We call that 'flipping the narrative'. Use some of the techniques I've outlined in the 'Comparison' list over the last couple of pages.

- Find someone who is a good, positive comparison – a role model. What is it that they DO that you would like to do? What are the things you can learn and that can spur you into action?

- You might even find someone you don't really like but who you do admire. This person is called 'a worthy rival' – someone who you might even want to beat, but in doing so, drives you to be better.

WE

- Encourage each other. If your friend is struggling with something, help them find an example of someone who has overcome the same issue as a way of helping them see there is hope.
- Be understanding to one another. When we start comparing people to each other, it doesn't consider the whole person. It just reduces them to the one thing we are comparing. We need to remind each other that we are all different; we have different strengths, and we are more than one label. Avoid using labels that are only around peoples' appearance, intelligence, style. Instead, you could find your own way of saying something like this: 'You got 90% in that test and I didn't this time. What did you do so I can learn and do better next time?'
- As a class, compare yourself to other classes as a way of creating positive action. For example, how much did the other class raise for charity? Beat it! How many praise points did that other class get? We will get more! What was the average score that class achieved on the test? We will score higher! Use comparison to help you do something positive. Everyone will feel the benefit.

We can recover from comparison-itus when we start thinking differently. We will always compare ourselves (it comes with being a human, I'm afraid) but, if we do it the right way, we will feel so much better about ourselves and the people around us.

Chapter 3
'He said, she said'

Do you ever find yourself telling someone else about an argument you have just had, and it is full of 'he said and then she said and then I said'? But realise that you haven't spoken to the person you have fallen out with to address it? Or found that the argument got bigger than you expected very quickly? If the answer is yes to these questions, join the club!

We are connected to the people who we live with, go to school with and socialise with, and we are all totally different unique people, so of course we are not always going to get along all the time. We all have our own (sometimes invisible) things going on that change how we feel or what we think too. It is not a surprise that sometimes we clash. But managing conflict and disagreements is something we must all do for the whole of our time on Earth, so it's time we got better at dealing with it.

Most of us hate conflict or arguments for a whole load of reasons:

- We don't like the emotions of it (sadness, guilt, shame, anxiety, regret).
- We don't like it when people don't like us.
- We are not good at thinking under (what feels like) an attack.
- We don't know how to put it right.
- We feel a bit paralysed trying to work out what to do about it.
- We don't want to make it worse.

Have a think about the last time you fell out with someone. How did you feel (even if you pretended to them that you weren't bothered)?

The nine Argument Traps

When we disagree with people, we can do it well or we can do it in a way that often makes things worse. We need to be able to tell people we are not happy or to disagree with them or to challenge something they have said without it getting heated and out of control.

'Argument Traps' are traps that we fall into, often driven by emotion and not by being calm. Some of them happen IN the argument and some happen AFTER it. When we start doing these things often, we make things more unpleasant and uncomfortable.

Look at this list of nine **Argument Traps** and think which of these you most regularly fall into:

1. **Being right so we tell the other person they are wrong**

   We might even sort of see their point, but we don't want to lose face, so we just keep arguing and dig our heels in. These arguments often happen with whoever we live with over the rules they are setting or the boundaries they have. Sometimes we must admit that we are wrong – sometimes we might not be! But going into an argument insisting that we are the holder of the only truth will wind people up.

2. **Talking / shouting over the other person (interrupting a lot!)**

   When we do this, it is like lighting a match and throwing it on to petrol. When we feel like we are not being listened to, it can cause us to get angry. When we don't take the time to listen to what someone is saying, then we can never really understand. In fact, we have no intention of understanding if we don't listen. It is hard to listen without interrupting but, if we can do it, it makes a difference.

3. **Working out what we are going to say next so we're not listening to them**

   Sometimes we put on our 'listening face' – you know the one! The one where our face says 'I'm listening to you' but our brain is planning our next swipe to take them down. We are listening to respond NOT listening to understand, and they are very different things.

4. **Blanking / ghosting them (even mid-argument)**

   This is infuriating and, if you have had this done to you, you will know how you responded. When someone just goes silent and looks away and refuses to talk, it may be because they are stopping themselves saying something they regret (which is good). However, most of the time it is a power move. Ignoring someone to hurt them deliberately, whether that is in the argument, in the corridor or at break, makes people feel invisible and often upset.

5. **Taking it on to social media (and making it worse and bigger)**

In schools, there are a lot of 'spill-over' issues that have come from social media. Arguments may not ever have happened in school, but happened last night online. The fallout then comes into school sometimes. The worst thing we can do after an argument is to take to a social-media platform and start venting. It is like throwing feathers into the wind: once they have been released, we can't get them back.

Our comments spread and cause damage, not just to the person we are attacking but also to US. LOTS of businesses now do social-media checks at interview stage to see our social-media footprint. Why? Because what we say, what we like, what we repost tells someone A LOT about us. More than we would ever realise. What may seem to you to be a good idea now in the heat of the moment may not seem quite as good when you're 21 and explaining yourself at a job interview. We might delete posts, but we have no idea who else has already seen it or what they have done with it.

6. **Saying hurtful things to try to 'win'**

This is a big trap that is so easy to fall into, but once we go here, it is hard to get back out. In the heat of the moment, sometimes we let our mouths run away with us and out pop things we don't even mean. We must control this better than we sometimes do. When I was a child, there was a popular rhyme that adults used to say if someone had been unkind to someone else. It is a ridiculous rhyme and totally untrue. It was, 'sticks and stones may break your bones, but words can never hurt you'.

I have no idea who came up with this phrase, but it is terrible on several levels. Of course words can hurt. A physical injury is horrendous and more physically obvious, but words burrow themselves into our brains and can stay with us for longer than they should, or than were ever intended. But let me be clear: BOTH are damaging. If I asked you now to tell me some words that someone said to you that hurt you, I bet you could, even if it was years ago.

7. **Doing something physical (rolling eyes, tutting, turning your back to them or walking off)**

This is the one that is particularly a problem when speaking to adults because it is perceived as a total lack of respect. In an argument, we emotionally leak, and it displays all over our faces. We need to be better at controlling our eyeballs in an argument. Rolling our eyes makes things significantly worse. Why? Because it says, 'you bore me, whatever, not listening, you're such an inconvenience, I have zero respect for you, when is this over? I have better things to do'. We may well feel these things inside, but we need to be better at being kinder and more respectful to people in these moments.

8. **Growing the argument so it started off as one thing and now it is about ten other things too!**

If we get caught by this trap, the more we do, the worse it gets. Perhaps you are discussing one specific thing, for example that you were upset at your friend's behaviour towards you yesterday. The conversation starts. You then take the chance to add a whole load of things to the list of complaints you have. 'I don't like what you said and it's not the only time you have upset me' and then what comes next is a big, long rant of OTHER things. Now you are in new territory, and this may not go well. It's now much bigger than the original issue.

9. **Saying sweeping generalisations, such as 'You *always*', 'You *never*'**

As soon as we start sentences with 'you', we are accusing people and they hear that. So perhaps you are arguing with the person who looks after you and they have missed what you just said because they were distracted. We might then say, 'You NEVER listen to me, you are ALWAYS ignoring me when I am speaking to you'. NEVER listen to you? ALWAYS ignoring you? Is that really true? (Maybe sometimes it is, but often it isn't.) We tend to say big, bold, general statements when we are arguing to cause maximum (negative) impact. And if we want things to get worse, the tactic will work. The other person will then defend themselves and then we are off into a bigger argument.

Like any trap, when we are caught in one we get stuck and can't get out of it easily (without usually feeling a bit bruised or injured). The best way to avoid a trap is not to get into one in the first place! So how do we do that?!

Arguments usually happen because something is wrong in the way someone has behaved, or we feel an emotion that is causing us some level of upset. Sometimes we sit on these things and then they explode out of us uncontrolled, and we fall into the nine Argument Traps.

There is a better way.

It is hard at first. It takes self-control, kindness, patience and a willingness to think the best of others rather than the worst BUT, when we get this right, we become bolder and braver. We have the confidence that we can handle tricky conversations.

We can try to avoid the traps and learn how to disagree well and to express how we are feeling without descending into an uncontrolled explosion. Here is how we can be better at disagreeing agreeably:

Four handy hints

1. **Think like a scientist.** Scientists don't just go by their emotions – they look for evidence, weigh things up and look at what the facts and data say. We should think about what we are going to say before we say it. What are the facts of this situation? Where is the evidence? There will be both facts and evidence, but make sure it is reliable enough to tackle. So, for example, if you want to talk to your friend because you feel they are ignoring you, what evidence will you give to back this up?

2. **Pause to get your brain in control.** Some research suggests that it takes 90 seconds to get from angry to more calm. When someone says something to you or you see something on your phone, try to take 90 seconds of pause before you act. In that 90 seconds, you have a chance to calm down and get your reactions under control. Look at your watch or timer and count 90 seconds: look at how little time it can take to get ourselves calmer. Do that whenever you can before responding. Your discussion may go better as a result.

3. **Focus on 'I' rather than 'you' sentences.** Rather than saying 'you made me feel' and 'you upset me', instead tell them how you felt, or what you thought you saw. Use the word 'I' – it is so much less threatening than 'you' because it is less accusatory and more honest and reflective. For example, instead of:

    'You deliberately upset me and left me out.'

    Say:

    'I felt upset because I felt like I had been left out.'

It's easier to blame other people, I know! We love using 'you' instead of 'I', but if we want to have healthier relationships then we have to get good at this. There is an activity on the next page in the 'Change your world' box that might help you.

4. **Have a 'go-to' structure that works.** Sometimes it is right that we talk to people about their behaviour towards us and how we have felt. But HOW do we have these conversations without it getting into an argument and getting out of control? This is the guide that I use all the time, and it works: Think of an issue you have with a friend / carer / family member and give it a go. BUT the whole thing should take only 60 seconds. This is not a rant or a monologue – this is to be said kindly, calmly and clearly. The aim is to talk and discuss without falling into any of the nine Argument Traps:

    a. **Name the issue.** Can I talk to you about what you wrote on [whatever platform] on Friday?

    b. **Select a specific example.** I read the comment that said '[insert comment]'.

    c. **Describe your emotions about this issue.** When I read it I was really upset, then felt really worried and couldn't sleep at the weekend because of it.

    d. **Clarify what is at stake.** I really want to be your friend, but also know that it feels weird at the moment and I don't want us to fall out.

    e. **Identify your contribution to this problem.** I'm sorry that I've been a bit weird with you for the last few days. I didn't know what to do and so I was avoiding you and I shouldn't have done – I'm sorry.

    f. **Indicate your wish to resolve the issue.** I really want to be friends and understand why you said what you said.

    g. **Invite the person to respond.** Sometimes this means you just stop talking after that last point and wait for them to speak in response to what you have just said.

    Then, we listen… and we avoid any of the Argument Traps! Why not have a go at this?

Being able to say hard things and have tough discussions without it going into a huge argument is a skill you will need for the rest of your life, not just now. You will need it in the future too, in your relationships and in the jobs that you eventually end up in. Get this right now, and you may save yourself a whole load of anxiety and maybe even heartbreak!

Change your world

ME

- Think of somebody who you need to have a conversation with because you know something isn't right. Go through the sentence starter. Remember that HOW you say it is just as important as WHAT you say: kind, calm, clear.
  1. Name the issue.
  2. Select a specific example.
  3. Describe your emotions about this issue.
  4. Clarify what is at stake.
  5. Identify your contribution to this problem.
  6. Indicate your wish to resolve the issue.
  7. Invite the person to respond.

- We have talked about not using 'you' sentences, but using 'I' sentences. In the sentences below, what Argument Traps can you see? Then try changing these YOU sentences to I ones.
  1. You are always having a go at me; you never stop!
  2. You say horrible things to me, and you don't care.
  3. You are wrong. And it's not just about this that you are wrong. I have loads of examples, for example [you can insert five more examples here!].

WE

- As a class, create an argument about something a bit silly, with made-up names and a fictional situation. Try to use as many of the Argument Traps as possible as you script it.

- Have a go at having this argument in a different way. Practise using the 'Four handy hints', and the model and the structure from the 'Me' section above.

Chapter 4
'Wait, what?!'

Everyone who talks, talks about other people. How much do we like it when the gossip is about us though? Perhaps not so much. But is all gossip bad?

According to research, not all gossip is bad. Before we start, we should define what we mean by gossip.

What exactly is gossip?

There are several definitions.

- The dictionary defines it as 'casual or unconstrained conversation or reports about other people, typically involving details that are not confirmed as being true'.

- Gossip is a conversation about someone who is not present.

There have been some studies done on gossip: who does it, what they do it about and how positive or negative it is. The box on the following page lists some of the findings.

FINDING 1: A study in 1993 found that males spent 55% of their conversation on socially relevant topics and females spent 67%.

FINDING 2: In another study in 2019, researchers found that, of the 52 minutes a day people gossiped for on average, three-quarters of that was neutral, NOT nasty.

FINDING 3: Robin Dunbar, who has studied this area, argues that gossiping helped our ancestors survive. Gossip is the equivalent of the primates picking flies or dirt off each other to connect to each other. We need it to connect.

FINDING 4: In a 2012 study, Matthew Feinberg found that, when people heard about another person's anti-social behaviour, or something that was an injustice, their heart rate increased. But when they were actively gossiping about the situation or the person, it calmed them, and their heart rates dropped.

Why might gossip be good?

You might not think that gossip can be good but, if we define gossip as talking about people who are not there, we do sometimes say neutral or even good things about those people. In fact, most of the time, we ARE saying neutral or good things. Studies found that, in a group of people who were observed, 75% of gossip was neutral: it was telling stories and exchanging information to feel connected. You might be talking about what happened in a lesson or talking about where your friend is or where someone went on holiday. None of that is negative, nasty or wrong.

Studies also found that 9% of gossip was positive. This kind builds people up, makes them feel great and celebrates other people's success. It might be telling someone that someone in your class or year has won a competition or has been selected to do something great. Again, this is positive and encouraging – there is no issue here.

When gossip is neutral or good, it can be very helpful.

Gossip can:

- help us feel connected and build friendships
- help us realise we are not on our own with our struggles

- make us feel less alone

- encourage us to process our thoughts better

- help us learn things about other people we didn't know.

If this was the only type of gossip that happened, then perhaps the world would be a happier place.

> **Have a think:** If you could come to school and know that there would only be positive or neutral gossip about you, how would that change how you felt?

The darker side of gossip

Studies showed that 16% of gossip is negative gossip. This is the kind of gossip that damages someone's reputation or changes their social position in some way. It is the kind that upsets people and has unpleasant consequences. It may be centred around someone's behaviour or physical appearance, and it usually involves criticism, verbal aggression and spreading rumours.

Although it seems a small percentage, it can cause significant hurt. You will know what I mean if you have ever been at the end of this. This kind of gossip can happen online as trolling or in person and turn into bullying. It isn't a gender issue either, despite what stereotypes might suggest. A study in 1995 showed that boys gossiped as much as girls.

Why do we sometimes do this?

This is an uncomfortable list to read, and we may not want to admit to some of it!

- Maybe we don't want to be excluded, and talking about someone else negatively makes us feel included.

- Perhaps talking negatively about someone stops their behaviour and brings them back in line with social norms.

- Maybe we find ourselves getting involved in negative gossip because everyone else is.

- Or perhaps (and we may not admit this) we occasionally want to cause other people to be hurt and upset. Maybe we want to get revenge, feel powerful or feel in control for whatever reason.

Whatever the reason we get into negative gossip, we need to know that no one benefits. Gossip and rumours damage our connection with each other, but they also mean that people won't trust us. If my friend is being nasty about someone else when they are not there, then how do I know they won't also be nasty about me when I am not there?

As we explored in Chapter 3, words can and do hurt. Psychologists who studied gossip among 7-year-olds found that one bad rumour is enough to make children suspicious and wary of each other. These same children trusted good rumours they heard if they heard them more than once from different people, but they were influenced by bad rumours they had heard only once. We may hear negative gossip, but it can have a bigger destructive impact.

Maybe the solution is simple? We don't believe all we hear if it is negative and we engage in negative gossip less (or maybe not at all!). That can be plan A and B, but plan C is how to handle it if you do start getting dragged into negative gossip.

Here are some things that can help:

1. **Ask for facts.** When someone tells you some negative gossip, don't believe it instantly. Ask for facts. It can be as simple as: 'How do you know that?', 'Are you sure that is true?'.

2. **Don't spread it.** Hearing it is bad enough, but it can stop with you. You don't have to pass it on and multiply the negativity, especially if you suspect it is not true. If what you hear is worrying you, you could tell a trusted adult and talk about it.

3. **Start positive or neutral gossip conversations instead.** Talk positively about people or talk about factual neutral information because we know that builds connection and helps us belong.

4. **Remove yourself from negative gossip.** We can walk away. Whether that is moving away from a group who are spreading negative gossip or not replying to chats online or even limiting how much time you spend on social media, sometimes distance helps.

Change your world

ME

- If you drew a pie chart of your conversations with your friends, how much would be positive, negative and neutral? What would you like to change about those figures on your chart?

- Have a look at the following statements. Which are positive, neutral and negative gossip? Copy the table, and work out which one is which and why.

	Gossip	Which type?	Why?
1.	Did you hear that Dani has gone on holiday and is missing two days of school?		
2.	Have you seen what he's done to his hair? It's awful. I'm surprised he's even coming in to school. You should see the pictures.		
3.	I went and saw the school play last night. Loads of people from our year were in it.		
4.	They've not done their homework for maths; they're all trying to catch up before the bell goes!		
5.	Did you hear he got in to the team? He found out last night and it's a big deal.		

WE

- We are connected. We can help each other and we can harm each other. When we talk in positive or neutral gossip, we help people feel safe, feel good and feel like they belong.

- Why not try your own research for a week and see what happens? If you all agree only to gossip positively and neutrally, how do you think each of you will feel at the end of the week?

- Agree together what the rules of this week are. Then try to live by them, together!

- Don't forget to review how it went at the end of the week!

  1. What did you notice about your conversations?

  2. What did you feel about being in this class?

  3. What did you learn about gossip?

Chapter 5
Here's the answer – what was the question?

Have you ever said the words 'YOU'RE NOT LISTENING TO ME!'? Most of us have. When we don't feel listened to, we may start getting angry. Although we have ways physically to hear, that doesn't mean we always listen! How can we do this better?

If you think about the recent arguments you have had, how many of these statements have you said?

- 'Will you just listen to me!'
- 'You're not listening!'
- 'That is not what I said!'
- 'You're putting words in my mouth!'
- 'Stop interrupting me!'

Perhaps you haven't said any of these things, but inside you felt an anger or a frustration that took over you and you walked off, shouted, went silent or said, 'just forget it' and gave up as you left.

The fact we have two ears and one mouth should probably tell us something important: we should listen twice as much as we speak. Yet many of us want to give people a good talking to and not a good listening to.

Why is it so hard for us to listen to others?

1. We want to interrupt with our own thoughts or advice (which we might think is better or more helpful!).

2. Sometimes we listen to reply and are not listening to what is being said.

3. We might get distracted and our mind wanders (or we are bored).

4. We like to talk about ourselves (because we find ourselves interesting!).

5. The person we are listening to is struggling and we want to jump in to make things better.

6. We think we know what the other person is thinking and so we feel we don't need to listen.

7. We feel that what we have to say is more important.

There are also lots of very good reasons why we WANT to be listened to:

1. We want to talk something through so we can work out what we think or feel.

2. We really want people to understand what we are saying.

3. We feel valued when someone gives us their full attention, without distractions.

4. We feel good when people are interested in what we think.

Have a think: Remember a time when you were trying to tell someone something that was important to you and they did not listen.

How did you know they were not listening?

Listening is a gift!

Like the best gifts, the gift of listening is one people want and a gift they appreciate. However, like buying a real gift, we need to show thoughtfulness, find the time, work out the cost and then plan when to give it. Sometimes we need to stop what we are doing and listen, so it costs us our time. At times, we need to put other people before ourselves and show people we value them by putting our plans on hold to listen to them too.

Giving real gifts can make us and the other person feel great; the same is true for the gift of listening.

Have a think: What happens to your ability to listen to someone when you are distracted by a screen? If your school has banned using phones at school, what have you noticed about your listening in school compared to outside of school?

The Listening Gift selection

There are lots of listening gifts that we can give. It is very likely that the more of them you give, the more positive the reaction of the person you give them to. It also feels great to be able to give this free gift too.

When we really listen and we 'get' what someone else is saying to us, something happens in our brains and in our hearts and we feel in sync. We are connected.

The Listening Gifts

You can try one or two of these Listening Gifts and it will make a difference with how connected you feel to others. The more you use, the better it is likely to be! Let me also tell you that many adults don't do this well at all. If you learn this now, you will be far better off in all areas of your life.

GIFT 1: Get rid of distractions (usually phones!). Beeps, pings and flashing devices: put them away! Focus on the person in front of you. Give someone the gift of your full attention. That is incredibly rare in today's world.

GIFT 2: Listen without interruption. Of course, you want to add encouraging noises that show you are listening, but don't interrupt with your thoughts when the other person is in full flow.

GIFT 3: Avoid 'boomerasking'. This is when you ask a question to someone so that the attention comes back to you, just like throwing a boomerang. This makes the conversation all about you instead of listening to the other person.

GIFT 4: Ask questions. Asking questions shows you are listening and helps you listen more. Sometimes the person speaking will find out new things about their own thinking when they answer your question, and you will find out more about them too! Ask questions that show you are listening though, for example: 'What happened after you scored that goal?'.

GIFT 5: Show don't tell. It is easy to say 'I'm listening, go on', but it is better to show them that you are listening. If you need to tell people you are listening, it is probably because you look like you are not! We show that we are listening by having eye contact or by nodding or using our bodies and faces to show that we are listening.

> **GIFT 6: Focus on what the person is saying – NOT on your reply.** If you spend the entire time thinking about what your next comment is, you won't be listening at all!

All of us can help people shine in the light of our attention. When we do, just notice what a difference it really makes.

Change your world

ME

Think about someone who you want to try to listen to better. Before you do that, think about:

1. What usually stops me listening to them?
2. What could I do next time to listen better?
3. What is the listening gift I find the hardest to give?

WE

Listening is hard, even though we think we know how to do it. Like anything that is hard, it takes practice to master it. Let's have a go at listening to each other in the class and see what it feels like.

1. Get into pairs. Label yourselves A and B.
2. A: You are going to talk for one minute without your partner interrupting you. If you run out of things to say, then B can ask you a question about what they have listened to. Your teacher will tell you when to start and will be timing you all.
3. B: You are going to listen to A. You are going to use the Listening Gifts.
4. At the end of a minute, swap over. Now B is going to speak and A will listen.
5. When both your minutes are up, discuss the following questions together:
   - How did it feel to be listened to?
   - How did it feel to be listening?
   - What was the hardest part of this activity?

Chapter 6
Them and us

Have you ever been in a group and looked at another group and felt like they are not the same as you? Perhaps you don't understand them? Don't agree with them? Or have even said nasty things about them? Sadly, this happens not just in your classroom or year group, but in society too. Why does this happen?

We like people who are like us. That is a fact from a lot of research. The 'Similar-To-Me Effect' means that we prefer people who look and / or think like us. We like things that are familiar to us too. Why do we think like this?

What some of the research says about the 'Similar-To-Me Effect':

FINDING 1: We treat people who we identify as part of our group better than those who are not in our group.

FINDING 2: We may think that our group is better than any other group and think our group is superior because we know them.

FINDING 3: People who are like us help us work out who we are; they become our 'in' group and we associate ourselves with them.

FINDING 4: We believe stereotypes. If we wear glasses and believe that those who wear glasses are intelligent, then when we meet someone with glasses, we make assumptions about them. This is the same when it comes to jobs, clothes, where people live and how people behave.

FINDING 5: People who are like us are comfortable to us; there is a shorthand that we feel we have already and so it feels easier to be around them. If it feels easier, we stick with the group because we might feel safer.

The problem with this is it can have some very big consequences. Here are six big consequences of the 'Similar-To-Me Effect'. We may do all these things to others AND we may also be the victim of the 'Similar-To-Me Effect' too.

Why the 'Similar-To-Me Effect' can be a problem:

1. **People may be biased in job interviews.** There have been some studies looking at job interviews. What they found was that, if the person doing the interview felt they were like the person being interviewed, then they thought the person was more suitable for the job. That might benefit us if we happen to be like the interviewer in some way, but it doesn't seem all that fair, does it?

2. **We may be more complimentary to one group over another.** Another report suggested that both men and women praise colleagues of their own gender more than those of a different gender. We seem to recognise the talent of people who are just like us!

3. **We can start showing prejudice towards others.** Being proud of where we live, or what we believe, or how we dress or what music we like is great. The problem is not about being proud of those things; the problem is when we start treating other people negatively because they don't believe those things. When we start to dislike, exclude, criticise or bully other people because they don't believe the same things, that's when it tips into something unpleasant.

   Sometimes we 'other' to make ourselves feel better or to define what we are not. This is a slippery slope if we are not careful though. Making ourselves feel good doesn't mean we have to make everyone else feel bad.

4. **Our wellbeing is affected too.** If we surround ourselves with people just like us then we know only the same things we already know. We can sometimes fall into the trap of something called 'confirmation bias'. This is when we give more weight to any evidence that supports what we already think. We might think, 'I think that too so it must be true!' It doesn't mean it is true though!

   We are attracted to evidence that backs us up instead of finding evidence that doesn't. If we keep recycling only what we already know, then we don't learn anything! Then it is harder to be creative, and it is more difficult to find solutions to problems. We don't have to agree with other people but, if we listen and consider their view, it makes us better too!

5. **We may start 'othering' people.** Sometimes, we think people like us are right, because they are like us and they may look the same

or believe the same things as us. What can happen is that we start viewing other people as wrong or less good than those in our group. Then we might look to the other group of people and label them. The label is probably not a nice one, and lumps all the people together in the same category.

As soon as we start using labels and making people separate from us, we start to see them as not as 'good' as us, and we group them together as one. We may even start seeing other people as less than human. When this happens, people justify in their own minds why they should treat that group badly. Then the bad treatment begins and, if we remove any reminder that these people are humans just like us, we act without guilt. That is when things take a terrible turn for the worse for all involved.

6. **We start seeing people as a group and not as individuals.** This can happen at a sports match where we say things like, 'the away fans were awful'. Perhaps a lot of them were badly behaved, but that doesn't mean every fan is badly behaved. There will be some who were and some who weren't. Big generalisations are not usually accurate. They can be helpful sometimes when we are describing generalities but, when we start categorising people and then implying that they 'all' do this or that, we risk being too simplistic in our attitude. Imagine you are in an assembly and a teacher says, 'this year group is badly behaved'. How do you feel if you haven't behaved badly? We must be careful about making sweeping statements.

> **Have a think:** Think about your friendship group.
> Is there anyone in there who is very different from you?

There are, however, some other reasons why the Similar-To-Me Effect can be helpful if used in the right way. If we use it in the following ways, then we can help empower and encourage others and help create connection.

Why the 'Similar-To-Me Effect' can be helpful:

1. **We can use the 'Similar-To-Me Effect' to help others be braver.** For example, if you are the only person who looks like you in an afterschool club, you might deliberately try to find other people like you so that they too can have the opportunities. This can be really empowering. If you see that you are the only boy in the dance class, you may want to find some other boys just like you to join you. If you are the only girl in the karate club, you might want to find some more girls to join you. When we do this, we open up opportunities for others and make people dream of what may be possible.

2. **We can use the 'Similar-To-Me Effect' to help ourselves.** If you have a best friend who is just like you, that can feel amazing. You will have things in common, be able to help and support each other, laugh together and trust each other. That can help you feel seen and heard and like you are connected to someone who 'gets you'. When we have these relationships, they are very important to us.

3. **We can use it to connect with other people quickly.** Chris Voss and Nicky Perfect were both hostage negotiators, and they talk about creating connections with people in a situation where things could get seriously out of control. They suggest we work out very quickly 'what have we got in common with this person?'. They find the common ground; it can be anything at all that builds a connection with the other person. It works to de-escalate tension and help people who are very different from us feel more connected to us.

   We can do that too: when we meet people who are different from us, we can find something we share. In some way, there will be something in them that is just like us – find it! It may be their age, their teacher, how many siblings they have, where they live, their taste in music, who they know who you also know, what subjects they like, what irritates them, what job they want to do in the future, their beliefs or what's on their birthday list.

There is so much more that we have in common. We are all human beings who go through all the same emotions at different times, and many of the same life events. We may be different in lots of other ways, but we will always have our humanity in common. What we need to do is to remember all that when we start looking at other people and finding ourselves tempted to try to de-humanise them.

We can benefit from people who are the same as us; we can also benefit from those who are totally different from us. We will be at a disadvantage if we don't open our minds and our hearts to others who have a different life experience from us.

Change your world

ME

- Think about the last week. Are there any examples that spring to mind of when you have made judgements about groups of people? You may have used a label that lumps people together all in one group. It could be saying things about the way people dress, or speak, or where they live or what they believe.

- How hard have you tried to find something you have in common with any of them?
- How often do you deliberately try to talk to someone who is not the same as you? Why not try this week? Find some common ground and talk about that.

WE

- Find a partner in your class who you don't know very well or who you don't normally hang around with or someone who you think is very different from you.
- On a sheet of paper, draw a Venn diagram like the one below. You may have come across them before at school. They help us see what is separate and what is overlapping.

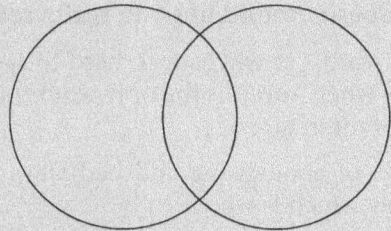

1. In one circle, write your name.
2. In the other circle, write your partner's name.
3. In the overlapping bit in the middle, you are going to write what you have in common with your partner.

Task

- Talk about as many things as possible with your partner, for example where you live, who is in your family, what your hobbies are, your favourite subjects at school, what your perfect holiday would be, what you would get for your birthday if you could have anything, your favourite computer game and your favourite team or music artist. If you have something in common, write it in the middle of the Venn diagram. If you like different things, write those things in your own circles.
- The aim is to find as much common ground in the middle as possible.
- Now look at your finished diagram. What do you notice?

Chapter 7
Sorry, not sorry

Have you ever been told to apologise and you don't want to? Or can't? Or don't think you should have to? Have you ever been told that the way you said sorry doesn't sound like you really are?

'Sorry.' Such a small word, yet why is it so hard to say? We find this time and time again. Even when 'sorry' is the only word that needs to be said, it is the last one some want to utter.

There are good ways of apologising and bad ways of apologising. It is helpful for us to know which is which.

Sorry, not sorry

Here are five ways people get this wrong:

1. **Placing the blame on someone else:** for example 'I'm sorry if you couldn't handle it' or 'I'm sorry if you were offended'. This type of apology sounds like one but isn't really. This person is not sorry for what they have done; they are putting all the emphasis on the other person. 'I'm sorry if you...' can imply that you did nothing wrong, but the other person is overreacting, and they are the one to blame. This can sometimes make things MUCH worse!

2. **Making excuses and getting defensive:** for example 'I'm sorry BUT...' – whatever comes after this 'but' is going to undo the apology. 'I'm sorry but it's not my fault', 'I'm sorry but you don't understand', 'I'm sorry but what about what they did?!'. 'BUT' can stand for 'Behold Underlying Truth'. In other words, whatever comes after that 'but' is what we really think. In this case, we are not taking responsibility and are finding someone else to share the blame or take it completely.

3. **Saying it in an angry and resentful way, getting sarcastic and then exaggerating:** for example 'I've said I'm sorry, alright?!' or 'What do you want me to do, turn back time? Let me just find my time-travel car and sort that out for you' or shouting, 'I'VE SAID SORRY ALREADY. WHY DO YOU KEEP GOING ON ABOUT IT?'.

4. **Thinking it is all or nothing – either apologise for the whole thing and be down on yourself or don't apologise at all and deny it:** for example 'I'm not sorry, it isn't my fault' or 'Sorry, all of this is my fault'. It IS possible to apologise for the part that IS your fault and take responsibility, for example 'I didn't realise that all that had happened – I am sorry I didn't realise because I wouldn't have wanted that to happen' or 'I'm sorry that I made that worse'.

5. **Insisting the other person apologises before you do:** for example 'I am not apologising until you say sorry to me!'. Someone has to go first – not to accept responsibility for everything, but to bring the argument or upset to a peaceful resolution as best you can.

Apologising is sometimes hard because we need to admit that we might be wrong or that we have caused hurt. We often don't like having to admit either of those things because it makes us feel awkward or vulnerable. Our ego is our sense of importance or self-esteem; admitting we have made a mistake can sometimes feel like we must admit we are not perfect and not always right. Even though we know that inside, it is hard to admit it to others. The good news is that there are no perfect humans: we all get things wrong, make mistakes and have regrets. Saying sorry is a part of being able to recover and move forward.

What do great apologies look like?

According to Roy Lewicki, lead author of the study on apologies at Fisher College of Business, there are six components to an apology if we want it to be a really effective one.

Researchers tested how 755 people reacted to apologies containing anywhere from one to six of the following elements:

1. **Expression of regret:** saying that you are sorry for what has happened

2. **Explanation of what went wrong:** briefly explaining why this has happened

3. **Acknowledgement of responsibility:** admitting that you are responsible for your behaviour

4. **Declaration of repentance:** apologising and being clear that you are sorry

5. **Offer of repair:** asking how you can fix the problem

6. **Request for forgiveness:** asking whether they will forgive you.

Although all are important, not all are equal. The research showed that the most important component is **acknowledging responsibility**. The second most important element is an **offer of repair**. People want to know that, not only do you take responsibility, but you are prepared to do something to fix what has gone wrong. People want action; not just empty words.

After these two crucial elements, the next three are all tied in terms of effectiveness: **expression of regret**, **explanation of what went wrong** and **declaration of repentance**. The least effective element is a **request for forgiveness**. If you must leave that out, apparently you can (and still have an effective apology!).

However, it isn't just the words that matter or the ingredients of an apology – you must mean what you're saying. The emotion and tone of voice of a spoken apology really are powerful. Eye contact, appropriate sincere expression and really meaning it (and looking like you do) are important.

Most of us don't like to be wrong. It takes humility and courage to say sorry and to make things right again but, if we can do that, then we will be able to connect better with others and be able to sort out tricky things.

> **Have a think:** Which part of this do you find the most challenging to do when you are apologising?

What if I am being apologised to?

We may be the one saying sorry or we may be the one who is receiving the apology. We need to make it easier for people to apologise by receiving it well. If someone is saying sorry, here are some ways we might want to receive it if we want to be kind, clear and gracious:

1. **Thank them for apologising, as it takes guts:** 'Thank you for your apology' or 'Thanks for saying sorry' or 'Thanks for acknowledging that I was upset.'

2. **Acknowledge that they have owned it:** 'Thanks for admitting that you made a mistake' or 'Thanks for coming to tell me – that must have been really hard' or 'Thanks for saying to me what you said'; you can say how you felt here: 'Thanks for admitting you said those things – I was really upset by it but it helps that you have seen that.'

3. **Forgive them and tell them you have:** These words are powerful and help close the issue: 'It's OK, I accept your apology' or 'I forgive you' or 'I want to put this behind us now.'

4. **Accept it and give them a way of getting back to normal (if appropriate):** This is when we offer something that they can accept to make things OK again – you may say: 'Shall we walk home tonight?' or 'Are we going to training tonight at the usual time?'.

Accepting apologies like this builds connection and helps repair disconnection. Taking someone's apology and turning it into our opportunity to have a rant about them, to them, probably won't help!

Change your world

ME

Looking at the six ingredients of saying sorry, which ones are you good at and which ones do you struggle with? As a reminder, they are:

1. Expression of regret
2. Explanation of what went wrong
3. Acknowledgement of responsibility
4. Declaration of repentance
5. Offer of repair
6. Request for forgiveness.

WE

- The apology recipe, made up of the six ingredients above, can also be boiled down to the 4Rs:

  - Recognition
  - Responsibility
  - Remorse
  - Repair.

- What do each of these words mean? Create your definitions and then look them up in a dictionary and see how accurate you were.

- As a class, write down what sentences would go under each step, so you think through your own examples. Then create an 'Apology Recipe' for your classroom. Remember all the techniques you will have learned in English too: write in the second person (you) and use recipe-related words like 'add', 'blend', 'sprinkle', 'leave' or 'mix'.

Chapter 8
Chatter-brain

Have you ever found that your brain starts firing off thoughts that seem to come from nowhere? Or that you have a voice in your head that tells you that you are stupid or you can't do something? Or you have silent conversations with yourself in your own mind? You are not strange; this is totally normal behaviour for humans. But sometimes this 'chatter' needs to be calmed or controlled.

Our brains are amazing things. Many psychologists have researched how the brain works and how we can better understand what it does and how it works so that we can get better at controlling it. One of these people is Ethan Kross, a psychologist who has written a book all about this, called *Chatter*. He outlines some things about the brain that would be helpful for us to know.

Did you know?

FACT 1: We have inner voices that are important to us.

When researchers have done studies on what we think about when our mouths are silent but our brains are active, we can see that there is a lot going on in there! We think about what we are seeing, like a constantly switched-on narration mode. We have thoughts that ping around all over the place from one topic to a totally different one. We think about ourselves a lot; what we think and what we feel. Our brains are undertaking this internal conversation, and it helps us make sense of the world and our experiences. It is a good reminder that, just because someone is quiet, does not mean that they don't have a very busy and chatty brain – they will have!

FACT 2: Even when we are asleep, our minds are at work.

Some of the most recent research suggests that our dreams are very much like the verbal thoughts we have during the day. Our sleeping brains are still processing and chatting and helping us to plan or to anticipate threats. Our sleeping chatter-brains are also helping us process who we are and what we are doing, which helps us create our identity.

FACT 3: We think faster than we can speak.

In fact, our brains are so quick that we can catch a falling object or quickly move out of the way of a reversing car before we are able to formulate the words to say what's even happening.

The average person speaks around 150 words per minute, but the average person is estimated to think at around 400 to 800 words per minute. Our brains can process information at a rapid speed. We can think much quicker than we can manage to articulate verbally. This is an incredible skill we have as humans: we can think fast and we can also speak, but sometimes those two things are out of sync!

FACT 4: Our brains can engage in time-travel.

Researchers have conducted research to see whether humans are the only ones who are able to think about the past, the present and the future. It seems that, currently, there is no convincing evidence that non-human animals can mentally time-travel like we can.

As humans, we can reflect on the past. We can take our minds back there when we lose something and want to retrace our steps or when we want to play over a past event. We can also think about the future and imagine different scenarios and then compare them to each other. We can enjoy being in the present when we are absorbed in something. Our brains jump in and out of all these different periods of time. We don't have an actual time machine, but the one in our heads is perhaps even more powerful.

Our brains are complex and we are too. Each of us has all that incredible capacity inside us every day; like our own control centre sitting in our heads. Sometimes though, our brains work against us. We all experience times when our brains start saying all kinds of things to us that might not be true and sometimes won't be kind.

We need to be able to engage in some mind control. When I was growing up, there was a magician called Uri Geller who said that he could get people to bend a metal spoon through the power of their minds. We watched on TV as the spoon seemed to bend. But no one bent a spoon just by thinking about it. It was a magic trick all along; a slight of hand and some distraction techniques.

We do need to engage in a different type of mind control though (without the spoons). If we do not control our minds, then we can end up believing what our brains are telling us... and sometimes our brains talk rubbish.

We need to learn some strategies to help manage our thoughts and to separate those thoughts that are helpful, constructive and positive from those that are unhelpful, destructive and negative. Although we cannot bend spoons, we can do much more than we might think to control our thoughts.

Brain talk

As well as being amazing, our brains can also shout quite loudly at us. When they start getting very loud, they can do all, or some, of the following:

- **Catastrophise:** we think about the worst possible version of the situation we are in and imagine all the terrible consequences that could happen

- **Argue with us:** our brains may tell us that everything we think is actually wrong, or that we are wrong or right, and then we might feel confused and don't know what to do

- **Criticise us:** our brains start telling us we have made a fool of ourselves, everyone is laughing and we are stupid

- **Go over things repeatedly:** we replay the same awful moment again and again but see more detail or different things, which can make things worse (or better, depending on what we are thinking about!)

- **Make us feel anxious:** the more we think about things, the bigger they can sometimes get, until we feel really stuck.

Have a think: When was the last time you felt any of these things? What was your brain saying and how did you feel?

When we experience these things, we may feel a range of emotions. Sometimes we even act out some of what is happening in our heads and our behaviour changes.

The good news is that we can learn to control the chatter in our heads so that we get the unhelpful stuff under control and maximise the helpful things. But we need to learn how, and the sooner we learn how, the more that managing our chatter can become part of our everyday lives.

When our brains are shouting things like, 'It's all going wrong!', 'You can't do it!', 'Just give up – no one believes in you' or 'This is the worst thing to have happened to you – you will never get over it', it's time to talk back.

These are some of the techniques we can use to talk back to our chatter-brains!

Stopping the chatter-attack:

TIP 1: Time-travel. This situation right now may feel terrible, so allow yourself to do some imaginary time-travel. Zoom yourself into the future, maybe one or five years ahead of now. Ask yourself, 'will this situation feel as bad then?'. The answer might be yes, in which case your brain may be having this reaction for a good reason. If the answer is 'no', then you can tell your brain that this is a problem for now, but it will pass. This brings perspective. It also helps us see that our emotional state won't last forever.

TIP 2: Talk to yourself in the second person. You will feel a bit mad doing this, so it might be better doing this on your own if you are going to do it out loud! If you feel yourself getting into a negative chatter cycle, talk to yourself and say, 'Look [add your name], you need to stop thinking like this. You can do it, you have done it before, you can manage this again and you need to start being more positive'. Giving yourself a pep talk can sometimes really help, just like a coach might give a half-time talk to their team. Sometimes you need to tell yourself to stop thinking like this; other times you need to be encouraging towards yourself and talk reassuringly. Research shows that people

---

who do this perform better under stress, think more wisely and feel less negative emotion.

TIP 3: Think in ink. Sometimes our brains are full of chatter, and we don't even know what they are saying – it just feels like a load of noise. One of the ways we can help to work out what we think is to 'think in ink', where we write down our thoughts. Marilyn Monroe was one person who used this idea, and many artists have used the technique since.

This isn't an assignment for English, so you don't need to write in full sentences, use punctuation or great vocabulary – you just need to write and see what comes out. What you write might surprise you and might help you work out what you think. You can tear it up afterwards or delete it from the computer, but sometimes it helps you make sense of things. For this exercise, often handwriting is even better than typing because it can help your stream of consciousness come out. Whether you type or handwrite, just have a try!

TIP 4: Get outside. Research shows that getting into green spaces or somewhere in nature can be helpful to get perspective. Not all of us live near green spaces, but there are still some things we can do. The sky at night is a great view to look at, with all those millions of stars, which can help us get perspective. Visiting the sea or a river, looking at trees or going to a park – maybe even just having a walk to get some fresh air – can help. We can also just watch a clip of nature; even that helps.

TIP 5: Avoid rumination. Having someone we can talk to so we can get our thoughts out can be helpful. It could be a teacher or another adult in school, someone in our family or a friend. Whoever we are talking to needs to listen and be supportive – just being heard can help. They need to be careful not to get into rumination with us though.

Rumination is what cows do. In the field, cows chew the grass and then it goes into their stomach and then they regurgitate it and bring it back up to chew it over again. On repeat! It is great for cows, but it can be terrible for humans. If our talking-things-through tips into bringing up the same thing repeatedly then we are not getting anywhere, and it may not be helpful at all. Sometimes we need a friend or trusted adult to say, 'we have gone through this problem, I hear you, but we need to find a solution now' or 'going over this repeatedly isn't helpful for you anymore: what is it you need to move forward?'.

TIP 6: Reframe your view. When we are about to do a test, meet new people or go somewhere unfamiliar, we can feel our hearts racing or feel a bit nervous or stressed. It would be easy not to do these things because of how we feel. What we can do instead is reframe things. That means, instead of saying, 'this is awful, I feel awful, I can't do it', we could think something different. We could remind ourselves that, when we feel like this, it isn't always our brains trying to upset us; it is our brains preparing us to perform well. Sweaty palms, quick breathing and a pounding heartbeat is our bodies' way of getting us prepared for a challenge.

Change your world

ME

There are so many things we can do to help our brains get under control. Some things really don't help us at all. Here are a few that research has shown *can* make things better. Look down the list and work out which one you are going to try.

- **Reduce your passive social-media use.** When you scroll looking for nothing, research shows that we don't feel calm or positive. How could you reduce your time just scrolling?
- **Try journalling.** Get a pad or a diary and just start writing: see how it feels!
- **Perform a ritual.** Lots of high-performing people do this; they have a set routine that helps them get calm. That might be packing your bag the night before school, checking you have a snack for break or reading a book or magazine before bed (instead of looking at a screen).

WE

There are many techniques that we can use to help each other:

- **Listen to people.** See Chapter 5 to remind you of tips on this.
- **Provide invisible support.** If you can sense that someone you live with is finding things stressful, they may not need your advice; they may just need you to pick up your clothes from the floor, tidy your room, put your litter in the bin or to let them sit on their own for a little while.
- **Perform a routine or ritual together.** Routines help us know that there is some order and control, especially if things feel uncertain. If you are in a team of any kind, you will probably do this already before a match because routines can help manage stress. What are your before-match routines? Maybe it is walking to school, when you build in routines such as agreeing what time someone calls for you, which way you walk or where you stop on the way. These predictable routines can create the calm order that our brains sometimes need.

If you are reading this as a class, what routines do you have together at certain times of the day, for example come in, coats off, equipment out, register? What else do you do? What else could you do?

Chapter 9
No laughing matter

Have you ever laughed so hard you were crying? Or got a case of the giggles that you just couldn't stop, no matter what you tried? I hope you have. It turns out that laughter like this is not just a laughing matter; it is also good for you. We would all be better off if we laughed more, but why?

There are some fascinating facts that have come from studies about laughter.

Did you know?

FACT 1: The average four-year-old laughs 300 times a day.

FACT 2: The average adult laughs only 15 times a day.

FACT 3: Research has shown that laughter reduces stress hormones (such as cortisol and epinephrine) and increases happy hormones (such as dopamine).

FACT 4: Laughter also increases the hormones that keep us healthy.

FACT 5: Laughter can even reduce pain.

FACT 6: Laughter improves blood flow to the heart, which results in greater relaxation and resistance to disease, as well as a better mood!

FACT 7: When we laugh, we are changed: we feel more optimistic and positive.

FACT 8: Laughter helps connect us to other people.

FACT 9: You can have a career in the scientific study of laughter and its effects on the body and mind: it is called *gelotology*.

Laughter is good for our health, but not just that: it is also important for friendships, families, schools and workplaces, but not all laughter helps. We really want the laughter that brings us together, not laughter that tears us apart.

When laughter isn't funny

There are some situations when laughter causes division, sadness and upset.

For example, when someone is laughing at us and it makes us feel embarrassed or ashamed, it isn't funny. When we are not part of the joke, or we feel that people are teasing or mimicking us or laughing at us to undermine us or be aggressive, then it can hurt. That is not humour; that is bullying, and we always need to ensure that our laughter is not destructive. People may laugh to hide what they are really feeling, but we need to be aware of the impact of our actions.

If we are laughing at something that someone else finds offensive, and they are offended, that is also destructive. We must live together in society. We can have different views and find different things funny, but we also need to be kind and considerate in how, when and to who we express our 'funny' remarks.

We don't want laughter to be a poison; we want our laughter to be a medicine. When we use laughter in the best way, it can help how we feel, both physically and emotionally.

The magic of laughter

There are lots of contexts where laughter works magic. How many of these have you experienced?

1. **We might think that we laugh at things that are funny, but studies show that we laugh more for social reasons in conversations.** We increase our chances of laughing by 30 times if we are with other people. Studies have shown an average of 7 laughs per 10 minutes of conversation between strangers. Even when we don't know people, we laugh a lot together. In our conversations with our friends, an average of 10% of the conversation is spent laughing.

2. **Laughter is contagious!** When we see someone yawn, we are also more likely to yawn. We are more likely to clap if someone near us is clapping. The same is the case for smiling and laughing; if someone

else is smiling or laughing, we catch it from them! These are known as *mirror neurons*; they are important when we are babies because we mirror what we see on other people's faces. Producers of sitcoms and panel shows use something called 'canned laughter', where people have been recorded laughing and the laughter track is played over the show. When we hear the laughter we laugh too, and so it is a popular technique in TV production.

3. **Telling jokes can help our careers.** According to research, people who can tell a good joke are seen as being more competent. There are even some studies that suggest that if a worker has a good sense of humour, they are more likely to be given more pay or a promotion! If you are someone who likes to laugh, tell jokes and help other people laugh then this is good news. BUT... this can also be risky. The humour we use should be short and simple and not offensive; it should also be appropriate to your audience. If you get this wrong, you will find that it goes wrong, quickly!

4. **Be able and willing to laugh at yourself.** This is called *self-deprecating humour*. It is where we make fun of ourselves or a mistake we have made. It can make people laugh and can help people see that we are not taking ourselves too seriously. When we are being light-hearted and gently mocking of ourselves then it is funny. We might need to be careful if we are being mean to ourselves: that is not funny for us or for other people to listen to or watch; it is just awkward!

5. **Laughter helps us connect with other people.** When we laugh together, for that moment, we are seeing the world in the same way. That might be in a classroom or a playground, in a shop or a park or at a concert or even watching something with other people. When we laugh together, we are connected to each other. We feel like we are similar, and that can be the start (or the reinforcing) of a new friendship. Research has found that, when we share a laugh (not just laughing generally), our relationships benefit the most.

6. **Laughter heals.** When we laugh, we feel safe. Laughter is to humans like tweeting is to birds. When we laugh, we are less stressed, feel calmer (even if we are hysterically laughing!) and it is good for our wellbeing. Laughter is a great medicine. William Fry (who was the original person who studied gelotology) referred to laughter as 'internal jogging' because it has some of the same impact as actual jogging! People who laugh every day have less chance of heart disease. For those in pain, watching a two-hour film that makes them laugh helps with pain relief.

There is even evidence that people with diabetes can also benefit from laughter through a lowering of blood-sugar levels.

Have a think: When was the last time you had a good laugh? Who was it with and how did it make you feel? Where do you not laugh as much? Why do you think that is?

Making it a laughing matter

We know that the right kind of laughter can give us lots of benefits, but how can we introduce more laughter into our lives? Here are some suggestions to try. The good news is that you don't have to be a comedian to do this.

1. **Tell stories.** When we simply tell people about our day or something that happened, we can laugh. We might be talking about what someone said or what we saw on TV and laugh over that.
2. **Tell jokes.** Learn some simple ones that are not offensive and try them out. People will laugh if they are funny and they may even laugh when they are terrible. We often call bad jokes 'dad jokes', which might be unfair to dads, but they still make us laugh.
3. **Laugh to connect before tough conversations.** Sometimes we can laugh about something small just before we have very serious conversations. This can reduce tension and awkwardness and make us feel more comfortable.
4. **Find moments to create laughter.** Whether it is being a bit silly, or exaggerating a story for dramatic effect, find ways of encouraging others to laugh. You could also try smiling at people more and see whether they smile back: that is a good start!

Change your world

ME

It is possible to work on laughter even if you are on your own. Why not try some of the following things?

- Find some funny films or programmes to watch.
- Find some jokes you like – they may be word puns or something else. Some of them are a bit cringy; others are clever, but find one you like. Here is one to get you going: 'I was wondering why the frisbee kept getting bigger and bigger, but then it hit me'.

- Try to make normal everyday things fun. See whether you can make your breakfast while standing only on one leg the whole time; try to eat your cereal with a fork, or other silly things, just because you can! All this gets us in the mood to laugh.
- Make yourself laugh out loud even if it is fake laughter to start with. This type of forced laughter counts too.

WE

Laughter is best enjoyed together because it helps us feel connected. We can do lots of things to laugh together.

- In English class, why not see whether you can write something funny and then read it out to each other. You could experiment with the 45 different humour techniques that appear in the book *The Art of Comedy Writing*.
- In tutor time, you could have a joke of the day and vote on them at the end of the week. Sometimes you will laugh because the joke is so terrible, but that is OK... you're still laughing.
- You could watch (an age- and content-appropriate!) comedy routine in tutor time and start the day by laughing.
- Watch a range of comedy styles and see which one gets the biggest laugh (and remember to laugh out loud and not stifle it!). Try programmes like *Miranda* or *Mr Bean* for slapstick comedy or *Horrible Histories* for exaggeration and caricature.
- Think about how you can make the people you live with laugh. Perhaps you can tell them a story about your day that will make them laugh or tell them the terrible joke you told in your class this morning.
- Just chat. The good news is that you don't have to crack jokes: just chat to each other and you will naturally laugh. Make time to chat (get off your screens!) and just notice how funny you all are naturally!

Chapter 10
Wishing and hoping

When you were younger (and maybe even now!), did people ask you to make a wish when you blew out the candles on your birthday cake? Or have you said, 'fingers crossed' as a way of saying 'I really hope this thing happens'. What's the difference between wishing for something and being optimistic that that thing will happen?

There is a big difference between wishing for something to happen and having certainty it will happen. I could say 'I wish I was a film star' but there is very little chance of that happening, and when I say that sentence everyone knows that what I mean is that it's a dream but probably not going to happen: it is fanciful thinking. If I say 'I am optimistic that I will be a film star', that sounds more certain – it sounds like I have reason for hope. But is there a difference between wishing and being optimistic?

What's in a word?

Words are fascinating. Sometimes the word we use is important. There are a lot of people studying the difference between a wish, a dream, a hope and then optimism. Let's start by understanding the definitions of these words:

- **Wish:** According to the *Oxford English Dictionary* online, it means 'to feel or express a strong desire or hope for something that cannot or probably will not happen'.

- **Dream:** This is a 'cherished aspiration, ambition, or ideal'.

- **Hope:** This is a 'feeling of expectation and desire for a particular thing to happen'.

- **Optimism:** This means a 'hopefulness and confidence about the future or the success of something'.

Have a think: What are the differences between these words now that you have seen the definitions? Which would you rather have: a wish, a dream, hope or optimism?

Rather like laughter in our last chapter, having hope or optimism also has amazing mental and physical benefits. A study in 2020 among 13,000 people found that a greater sense of hope was linked with:

- reduced all-cause mortality (reduced death rates!)
- fewer serious health conditions
- lower risk of cancer
- fewer issues with sleep
- increased positive mindset
- better sense of life satisfaction
- maintaining a sense of purpose in life
- less distress in the mind
- better social wellbeing.

That is quite a list, isn't it? If we have hope and optimism, then we have confidence and belief that success is possible and so is a positive future. Do you know if you are an optimist? In the table below are some of the personal traits that optimistic people tend to have. Copy the list and tick the ones that you think apply to you.

Number	Optimistic trait	Is this me?
1.	I believe that good things are coming.	
2.	Even when things are a challenge, I believe they will somehow work out OK in the end.	
3.	In uncertain times, I usually expect the best.	
4.	I am usually optimistic about my future.	
5.	Overall, I expect more good things to happen to me than bad.	
6.	I feel gratitude for the small things in my life.	
7.	I know that a bad day doesn't mean a bad everything.	
8.	I have a positive attitude towards myself and others.	

How do people become optimists?

The research isn't totally clear on this, but there are lots of factors that contribute to being an optimist. It can be partly our genetics (around 25% apparently), our upbringing, the culture in which we live, our life experiences so far and lots of other factors about our environments. The good news for you is that a study found that the optimism levels of young people increase through their teenage years and early adulthood. So, there is lots to look forward to (an optimist would say!).

You may have heard people say, 'is the glass half full or half empty?'. This is a question about optimism. If you see a pint glass half full of Diet Coke sitting on the table in the school dining room, would you say, 'that glass is half full' or would you look at it and see all the empty space remaining in the glass where Diet Coke could have been and say, 'that glass is half empty'?

How we describe the glass, or our lives, can tell us something about whether we might be an optimist or a pessimist (the opposite of an optimist). We all tell ourselves stories to make sense of our world; it so happens that this story is really very important.

The story we tell ourselves

'The story we tell ourselves' is about the way we explain the events that happen to us. There are three questions we can ask ourselves:

1. **Is this situation permanent?** In other words, is this going to be long-lasting?
2. **Is this situation pervasive?** If something is pervasive, we think it impacts everything, so is this situation going to impact my whole life?
3. **Is this situation personal?** Are events caused by me or an external force?

Let's see what this looks like if we think optimistically and then if we think pessimistically.

Let's imagine that you have done a test and you got a bad mark.

If you are thinking like an **optimist**, you will answer the 3Ps like this:

1. 'This is not permanent; it is temporary. It is one test. I can revise, ask for help and then do better on the next one if I work harder. This situation can be changed.'
2. 'This is not pervasive; it is a specific moment. This is disappointing right now, but I will be able to put this right next time. This isn't going to ruin everything else.'

3. 'This is something I can do something about and change. Some of the questions set were tricky but I know that, with more preparation, I can get a different outcome.'

If you think like a **pessimist**, you might take the opposite view, saying things like:

1. 'This test mark is going to ruin every future opportunity that I wanted.'
2. 'I never get good marks in tests.'
3. 'It's all my fault – I can't do it, and there's nothing I can do.'

Now, of course, both pessimists and optimists are putting their own spin on things; one more positively than the other. The good place to be is to be a realist. Realists see things clearly – they don't label things as positive or negative; they just see what is, not how they want things to be. Most of us find it hard to be realists because we have emotions and thoughts that lean towards us being more positive or more negative in our thinking.

Have a think: Which one do you think you are most of the time? Think about a situation you have faced recently. Where did your thinking lead you: to thinking the situation was permanent, pervasive and personal OR that it was temporary, specific and external?

There is good news!

In fact, it isn't good; it's great. We can all change our thinking. But how?!

1. **We can become our own detectives.** We can question ourselves and find the facts. Think of yourself as taking the role of a detective who wants to get to the bottom of the situation. When something difficult happens, get your inner detective to ask yourself the questions we looked at earlier:

   a. **Is this permanent or temporary?** (Remember: we are looking for facts!)

   b. **Is this pervasive or specific?** (Your brain may tell you it is pervasive, but just check whether the facts agree with that!)

   c. **Is this personal or external?** (Is this something I could have controlled or is this beyond my control? Remember: we are looking for facts, not just opinions or feelings.)

2. **We can become our own cheerleaders.** Sometimes when we start thinking pessimistically, we have to have a word with ourselves and

start speaking positively to ourselves. We covered this in Chapter 8 about chatter-brain, and it really is important. If a test you have done gets a bad mark, you might say, 'I failed this test because I am stupid': that is a pessimistic view. How can we turn that negative phrase into something more optimistic? 'I now know the areas I need to work on so that I can work hard and get better marks next time.' Perhaps we can attribute it to external factors too: 'I didn't do well on the test because there was so much noise next door last night that I couldn't sleep and so tiredness caused me not to concentrate as well as normal'.

3. **We can become coaches for others.** When our friends or families slip into feeling pessimistic, we can model what optimism looks like. We can ask the questions we have asked ourselves: is this permanent, pervasive or personal? Sometimes, when we get ourselves into a downward spiral, someone else can help us find our own way out by asking great questions.

4. **We can become advanced planners.** If we were going on a journey, we would usually plan how we would get there, what might go wrong and how we would overcome those things. We can do this for other things too. We can think ahead to situations and decide in advance how we might handle them. For example, if we know we have a test coming up, we might think, 'How am I going to view this test: as something that will change my life forever or as something that will help me work out what I don't know and can't do so that I can then learn it?'. Sometimes, we can take the pressure off ourselves by thinking differently and in advance.

5. **We can become action heroes.** I don't mean the ones with capes and special powers, of course. What I mean is that we can decide that we can change something that we see is wrong and refuse to believe it is permanent. For example, we might have noticed that our local area is covered in litter and looks a mess and uncared for. If we take a pessimistic view, we might say things like, 'This is always going to be like this; there is nothing that we can do and it just shows that everyone hates us and this area'. Or we can say, 'This wasn't always like this, and the litter isn't permanent if we pick it up. If we start doing something, we could encourage other people to make a change. We can start to help people be proud of our area'. All that takes is a bin bag, a litter picker and a different outlook.

6. **We can get ourselves in the driving seat.** We can start to believe that we have more control than we think. We can't control things like the length of our lessons or the timetable or who teaches us or when the tests

are. We also can't control what other people think and feel or how they behave. However, we CAN control how much we concentrate, what our work looks like, how much we listen, how many questions we ask, how hard we work and whether we complete homework. We can also control how *we* think and feel and how *we* behave. The more things we can see that we can control and influence, the more optimistic we may feel!

You have more power than you might think. There are so many young people who have done something to change the way their school works, or fix a problem in their town or raise money for charity (which literally can save lives).

Change your world

ME

- We need to practise flipping our narratives and creating a better story. The table below shows you what optimistic and pessimistic thinking says on a specific situation. You are going to try filling it in with your own situation.

	GOOD situation *You get a positive praise point for completing your homework.*	BAD situation *You do not get a positive praise point for completing your homework.*
Optimist	• It's great that my work has been recognised. • I always work hard, which is why this has been recognised. • I am organised and hard-working, which is why I get my homework done.	• If I keep doing what I'm doing, they will eventually give me a praise point, I'm sure. I can't get one every time anyway! • It's good that they give different people recognition. • I think they probably have to choose different people each week to make it fair and it just wasn't my turn yet.
Pessimist	• I've got this praise point now, but I bet they never give me one again. • Just because they have given me this now doesn't mean they think I deserve it. • Everyone got one so it isn't anything to do with me. It's just a fluke.	• Typical: they never see my effort, and so what's the point? • I won't get one in anything now and then everyone will think I'm not as good as anyone else. • It's my fault I didn't get one because I don't do anything as well as everyone else. They hate me.

- Now have a go at copying the table and filling it in with a different situation.

	GOOD situation *Situation:*	BAD situation *Situation:*
Optimist	• Permanent: • Pervasive: • Personal:	• Temporary: • Specific: • External cause:
Pessimist	• Temporary: • Specific: • External cause:	• Permanent: • Pervasive: • Personal:

WE

- Draw outlines of two people. Annotate the first person with all the things you can control and then annotate the second person with all the things you cannot control. As a class, think about the things you can control and the things you can't. Psychologists call this a 'locus of control'. It's basically a scientific way of describing what you believe about who is in control. Do you believe YOU are in control and can make things happen? Or do you believe other people are in control and things happen TO you?

- If you have an internal locus of control, you make things happen. As a class, what can you make happen? What can you control?

- If you have an external locus of control, things happen to you. As a class, what can you not control? What decisions are made for you and done to you?

Chapter 11
Kicking the habit

Have you ever wanted to start a new habit but then found it hard to do? Perhaps it is making sure you pack your school bag the night before, do your homework in enough time or revise for a test? Or perhaps you want to get out of some bad habits, like constantly checking your phone or trying not to have the same thing for lunch every day! Learning about how we form good habits, and break bad ones, is an important thing for us to know.

The first thing to know about habits is that they have become a money-making goldmine. In fact, many companies are better at getting us to form habits than we are. What do I mean by that? Well, many companies are fighting for our attention, and they know how to get us hooked. They know that the longer we stay on their apps, the more money they can make. They might have adverts to sell to us, or they encourage us to buy more by 'unlocking' levels or prizes. The longer we are on an app, the more information the companies are finding out about us and, of course, they can then use that information to get more of our attention.

But this whole thing works only if companies can encourage all of us to use apps compulsively and get us into the habit of being online more often and for longer.

Getting hooked

According to psychologist and author Nir Eyal, social-media companies use the 'Hooked Model', which is a four-stage model to help get you hooked.

The Hooked Model

1. **Trigger:** This is the spark that starts it all. We may see a notification or a picture, get an email, see an update from a friend, see we have a message, and all that makes us want to get into the app to check. Sometimes we take the trigger because we are intrigued, but sometimes it is just that we are bored: we reach for the phone or tablet and start scrolling; that is enough to start a digital habit.

2. **Action:** When the trigger has worked to get us in the app, now the companies are fighting to get our attention and get us to start clicking. We might like something or share, post a picture, comment or click on a link that takes us to another app, and then we start getting content pushed to us, which we start watching. This is how companies get us to stay on the apps longer to see more content. The key thing here is that these actions must be easy and require minimal effort from us.

3. **Variable reward:** When we are scrolling, lots of things don't interest us and so we might swipe past them quickly, but then every now and again a cute animal video or a funny video comes up, and our effort is rewarded. We stop, and we look. Our effort has been 'rewarded' and we get a hit of the hormone dopamine, which impacts our mood. We have no idea whether or not we are going to find a funny puppy video, but the thought that we might is what keeps us coming back for more.

4. **Investment:** The companies know that, if they are going to keep our attention, they must encourage us to invest. This is made really easy; we can create groups or give feedback or try certain new features (or special gifts or rewards) that are 'unlocked' especially for us. We can build our own avatars, earn the ability to win points to dress up our avatars or personalise our stories or our filters. We can like and dislike things or express a range of other emotions. When we like, dislike or share, the companies learn things about us and then they can give us more of that thing… because that is likely to keep us there longer.

Clearly, these big companies have understood so much about human psychology and behaviour that they can now use that knowledge to manipulate us, change our behaviour and get us hooked in. Getting us into a habit means that other people benefit.

It isn't all bad, of course. Some companies use the same psychology to get us into good habits that will really help us. In fact, your schools may be encouraging you to use apps that help create good learning habits because they have seen the benefit of them. Whether that is a multiplication or maths app, a language-learning app, a quizzing app or an app to learn key facts in each subject, if we do this every day and develop habits that keep us going on to the apps, we will benefit. Using these things every day means that our knowledge will be greater, our learning will be stronger and our academic achievement will be higher. In these cases, our habits are going to help us too.

Have a think:

Which apps do you use that help your learning and give you good habits that will benefit you?

Which apps or games are you on where you get into a habit, but it may not be good for you?

How can you tell the difference?

Can we be as clever as these big companies?

These companies know how to tap into our brains and help us develop habits. The great news is that we can learn this too and then start doing this for ourselves.

So here is a brief overview of how you can create great habits for yourself and break bad ones. Like everything else in this book, if you can do this it will put you at a significant advantage in your life; not just for school, but for work too (when you get there!).

Creating GOOD habits for ourselves

Our habits tell us a lot about our lives, and make up about 40% of our behaviours each day, according to the researchers at Duke University. Habits are what we think about and what we do every single day. Habits affect how happy we are, how healthy we are and how successful we are.

There are some stages involved in creating good habits, and these stages help habits stick.

Good habit stages

Let's imagine that the good habit we want to create is to do our homework on the day that we get it. The following list, by James Clear, author of Atomic Habits, explains the good habit stages, along with some things we could do to get the homework done and develop good habits every day.

1. **Make it OBVIOUS.** We need to put some obvious reminders in, called *cues*, so they are right in our faces. How can we make doing this homework obvious?

   - We might write it clearly in our planner when it is set.

   - The online platform might send us a reminder that evening.

   - We could set a reminder in our phones or our carers' phones.

   - We could stick a note on the snack tin at home!

   - We could agree with the people who we live with when we are going to do this.

   - We could make sure we always have the right equipment available ahead of time (even a drink and a biscuit ready on the table!).

   - We could link it with another habit, such as 'I will come in from school, eat a biscuit and have a drink and then sit in the kitchen to start my homework'.

2. **Make it ATTRACTIVE.** We need to make homework feel like an attractive thing to do. We could do that by:

   - having a 'planthem' – this is a favourite song that helps us get into the mood to do the thing we need to do

   - agreeing what the reward is if we do this (I don't necessarily mean money here, before you get excited: it could be extra time playing a game or seeing friends or having free time to do what we want) – eventually the reward is in doing the thing, because we start feeling good that we have done it, and that is addictive (remember dopamine from earlier!)

   - reframing our language: instead of 'I HAVE to do my homework', say 'I GET TO do my homework, and there are many people who would love to have this chance and don't have it'

   - agreeing with our friends that we will all message each other when we have all done it, creating a positive team habit

   - agreeing with ourselves, if we have some sweets, that we can eat one every 10 minutes or after every question we answer!

   - having a tick chart (a bit like the rewards chart you may have had when you were younger when your carers were potty-training you!) – they do work; make yourself a chart and tick each day you do this routine and see the success build up.

3. **Make it EASY.** We must make doing homework as easy as possible so that we don't give up, especially when it gets tricky. Here are some ways to make doing your homework easy!

- Be in a room where there are no distractions!

- Ask your carers to hide the remote controls until the work is done.

- Start small. Don't try and do three hours of homework in one go; start with two to five minutes.

- Do your homework in the same place each time so you start associating that place with this task.

- Make sure you have any equipment charged and that, if you share a device, others know you need it at this time and for this long.

- Stay at school and do it… you're already there!

4. **Make it SATISFYING.** We need to get some form of payoff so that we feel that it has been satisfying. The payoff can be a reward, or it can be knowing that we are moving towards an identity we want to have. For doing your homework, some of these might help:

- Lead with who you are becoming first. For example, when you do science homework, you are a scientist. When you do English homework, you are a writer.

- Find a physical way of tracking your progress; put a marble in a jar every time you do your homework and then, when the jar is filled, decide what your reward will be (it doesn't have to be an expensive one!). You might print out a month's calendar and tick off each day of doing homework; aim not to break the chain. Seinfeld, an American comedian who wrote a TV series of the same name, used this technique to write funny jokes each day.

- There is a technique called 'temptation bundling', where you do something you have to do and then link it to something you want to do. For example, after I have done my 25 minutes of maths, I will watch 20 minutes of the series I was watching on Netflix.

You can take any habit that you want to develop and try these techniques. It works, but only if you do it and don't just plan it!

Alongside developing good habits, we also need to stop some bad habits. How do we do that? According to many psychologists, we just flip what we do to develop good habits.

Breaking bad habits

Bad habits describe those things that we keep doing but know they are not helping us. This might be to do with elements of our behaviour or how we spend our time.

Think about a bad habit you want to break. Then ask yourself these questions:

1. How can I make this invisible?
2. How can I make this unattractive?
3. How can I make this difficult?
4. How can I make this unsatisfying?

If you ever feel like you can't do something, perhaps ask yourself how your bad habits might be stopping you and how developing good habits could change your circumstances. You have more control than perhaps you realise: use it well!

Change your world

ME

- Have a think about all the good habits that you have. How do you keep doing them?
- Now have a think about the habits that you think might be bad. What would you like to change? What could you do to break these habits?

WE

- As a class, we may also have habits that are good and bad. Think about the following times in school and write down the good habits and bad habits in those times:
  - Coming into the class in the morning
  - Breaktimes
  - Getting and eating lunch
  - The start of lessons
- Pick one from the list above and suggest two things that you could do to have better habits.

Chapter 12
Who cares what people think?

Have you ever worried what people think of you? Perhaps you have panicked over what you're wearing for non-uniform day or what people think of your new hairstyle. Someone close to you may have heard your worry and said, 'who cares what people think?'. But is caring what people think always a bad thing? Are there times when it is helpful to care what people think? Are there times when caring too much is a problem?

To care or not to care?

This is the question we need to think about. It is one of those issues where there is nuance. *Nuance* means 'a subtle difference in or shade of meaning, expression or sound'. When we are looking at issues like this, we should look at those very subtle differences of thought and not just jump to 'yes' or 'no' answers.

Have a think: Look at the following scenarios. Do you think the person doing these things should or should not care what people think?

- A member of your class is being disruptive by deliberately misbehaving, which means the teaching and the learning is being disrupted. Should they care what people think?

- On non-uniform day, a person wears something that they are proud to wear because it is how they want to look and they do not look the same as others. Should they care what people think?

- A person is playing in a sport's match, and a talent scout is coming to watch the game to spot people who could get a scholarship. Should the player care what people think?

- On a bus, a person is playing loud music on their phone. The songs have some explicit lyrics in them. There are small children on the bus. Should the person playing the song care what people think?

- Someone likes a music artist that most people haven't heard of. Should they care what people think about this?

- A group of teenagers are mucking around late at night outside a residential care home. Should the group care what people think?

- A person at school has views that are offensive to other people in the class. Should the person with the views care what these other people think?

This may have been tricker than you imagined. But why might it have been trickier?

Perhaps you think that we should all be able to do what we want no matter what others think? Or maybe you think that we should just fit in with what other people are doing and if everyone is doing it, it's OK? Maybe you think if something makes you happy, you should be able to do it, even if it makes everyone else miserable? Or maybe you think that we should always care what people think and we should change what we like or think just to fit in?

You might think different things at different times. That is because many of these things depend on contextual information.

When is caring what people think helpful for us?

Here are some of the ways that caring what other people think can be a good thing for us and for our lives.

1. **When we want to improve:** If we want to improve at something, it is helpful to know what people think of our work or performance and what we might need to work on. If we want to improve, it would be very arrogant not to care what people think, especially when others might be able to help us improve. They may also know things we do not yet know.

2. **When we are leading:** If we are leading a team, it is helpful to know whether those people are enjoying being led by us; their opinion helps

us make changes. If we are the boss and our team really hate working for us and are trying to leave, we should care about them and what they think.

3. **When we are in relationships:** If we are causing people damage, hurt or stress, it is helpful to know how they feel so we can choose to shift our behaviour and change. If we are causing someone to be sad and don't even care, then that might be the end of a friendship or a relationship. Part of loving someone (as a friend or in a romantic relationship) is that we want to listen to and understand their views and make things better for them, because that is a big part of love.

4. **When we need confidence:** If we have low confidence, it can be important to know what people think because it encourages us and helps us not give up. People might see something in us that we haven't seen in ourselves and so, if we care what they think, we might start believing more in ourselves.

5. **When we want success:** If we have anything we are selling, we really want to know what people think. For example, if we are a music artist producing our latest album, we really want to care what people think. When Pixar produce movies, they gather a group of people together and call them the Brain Trust. The job of the Brain Trust is to tell the writer what they think of their film; they ask questions, make comments and make suggestions. The writer doesn't have to act on all these things, but they would be foolish not to consider them if they want the film to be successful.

6. **When we want to understand others:** Henry Ford (who invented Ford cars) said, 'if there is any one secret to success, it lies in the ability to get the other person's point of view and see things from their angle as well as your own'. If we are trying to resolve an argument, create world peace or work out where a situation has gone wrong in the first place, we must care about the views of others. It doesn't mean we have to agree with or believe what they say, but we must care enough about their views to ask them what they are!

7. **When we belong to a community:** We all belong to at least one community: our school. Communities stay orderly when we all care a little about what other people think. Imagine if I decided that I don't care what other people think or care about the rules and so I decide to drive through a red traffic light. I don't care whether people are honking their horns because I am expressing myself. Imagine the total chaos, danger and anxiety that would create! If we want to live in a

safe and harmonious community, there are some things we just don't do because we care about the rules and about what people think if we break them. If in school we are disrupting other people's learning, we should care about what our classmates think, and what our teacher thinks too. The behaviour we're choosing might well be stopping other people concentrating, which may stop them doing well, which may well impact their future. We all should care about that. Not to care in this situation is being selfish; caring more about ourselves than about others.

When is caring what people think unhelpful for us?

There are times when caring too much can cause some issues. Here are some of them:

1. **If we care so much what people think that we live in fear:** This can happen in all kinds of circumstances. What will people think of my trainers? What will people think if I don't do well in the test? What will people do if they find out what my hobby is because no one else does it? What if people don't want to be my friend? You might have had some of these worry attacks. When we worry about people judging us or rejecting us, it can make us worried about what they think and that can make us feel really stuck and scared.

2. **If we change what we think or feel to fit in:** This can sometimes be helpful in some contexts (as I mention earlier – remember: this is nuanced). However, if we are pretending to change what we think or feel so that we 'fit in' and go under the radar, that doesn't always feel good. We don't have to give up things that make us who we are because other people might not get it. Every single one of us is unique and we should celebrate that; you are the only one of you that exists in the entire world. You are a limited edition! When we squash down the things that make us feel joy because we care what other people think about that thing, we may need to think again!

3. **If we become people pleasers:** This is when we are so worried what people think of us that we change how we behave to try to control the emotions of the other person, so that they will think better of us. So, let's imagine I am worried that people think I am boring or unpopular and, because I want them to think I am fun or popular, I now do something whacky (that I probably don't really want to do) so that they think I am fun, cool or popular. What happens then? I do the thing I don't really want to do. They might think I am fun, cool

or popular. I have managed to manipulate them into thinking I am something that I'm not, all so that they like me and I feel better about myself. This happens more then we might think in humans of all ages! When we fear rejection, sometimes we end up hiding who we are to our detriment.

4. **When we care what people think and come to the wrong conclusion:** We may look at someone in our class and think 'they don't care what people think', but it is highly likely they do; they may just be disguising it well. Sometimes we imagine what people think about us, without any evidence that this is true. You may have heard yourself think things like, 'I bet they think that I'm stupid' or 'I reckon they think that I'm weird'. While we are thinking these things, we are going to start pretending, or distancing ourselves from them, or we feel sensitive and vulnerable. Then, sometimes, we start hiding ourselves from people. We can start to feel invisible. All this has happened in our own heads because we care what we think people think!

We have gone through some of the reasons why we shouldn't care as much what people think, and then why we should! Both things can be true at the same time, even though it looks like they contradict each other.

What can we do to get the right balance? We must live in the heart of the paradox. A *paradox* is when something sounds like it is contradictory but can also be true.

Have a think: Where are you on this line? Copy the line and put a little x to mark the spot!

I care too little what people think.

The sweet spot: I can both care what people think and not care what people think, depending on the context.

I care too much what people think.

Ideally, if we were all in the sweet spot in the middle of this line, we might find that we are happier, more content and more able to be ourselves. We would also be able to show empathy and compassion towards others, to see where people are coming from and to adjust our behaviour or thoughts, if appropriate.

How can we live in this sweet spot?

Here are some ways that we can move more to the middle of this line.

TIP 1: Surround yourself with people who want to interact with the real you. Go to clubs or join teams where you can meet other people who like the same things as you. When we do this, we feel like we belong, which is far more than just fitting in.

TIP 2: Ask yourself a change-checking question before you change anything! When you are tempted to change something because of what others might think, ask yourself, 'Is there a good reason to think that they will even think this?' and 'Is their opinion of me a good enough reason to change?'. Sometimes the answer may be 'yes' and other times the answer will be 'no'. Then ask, 'What are the consequences of me doing this?'. Just check with yourself before you do the change!

TIP 3: If you are worried about someone rejecting you or being judgemental, ask yourself, 'What am I scared of if this happens?'. Are these fears realistic concerns? As you already know, our brains sometimes talk rubbish and our internal chatter-brains bombard our heads with thoughts that may not even be true. Sometimes we feel stuck because we are fearful of something, but sometimes, rather like the imaginary monster under the bed, there is nothing to fear.

TIP 4: If you behave in a way that is kind and considerate, then there is far less need to worry what everyone else is thinking in the first place as your behaviour will be thoughtful. Some studies show that when people consistently think of others, rather than themselves, they are more successful, so there are benefits of being a giver, rather than a taker. For example, if you can override your selfish impulses, using your willpower becomes easier. If we are other-centred instead of self-centred, it helps our own willpower and motivation, but also helps us see things in different ways.

A study showed what happened when two different signs were put up at hospital handwashing stations to encourage people to be careful about hygiene. The first sign said 'hand hygiene prevents you from catching diseases' and the other said 'hand hygiene prevents patients from catching diseases'. The researchers measured the amount of soap used at each station: at the station with the sign about patient hygiene, doctors and nurses used 45% more soap or hand sanitiser. This is called pro-social motivation and it can benefit us AND others!

TIP 5: Develop 'attentional control'. This is when we control what we are paying attention to. Some people find mindfulness helps with this, where we might pray, meditate, think about what we are grateful for, journal or do some breathing exercises to refocus our attention. Other people find that the best thing to do is to jump into action. Choose actions that are pro-social though, like writing someone a card or letter or doing a random act of kindness to make you and someone else smile.

Change your world

ME

Have a go at answering these questions so that you can understand how your mind works:

1. If I worry about what people think, whose opinions bother me the most and why?
2. If I could wave a magic wand and instantly find myself living in the sweet spot mentioned, how would my life be different?
3. Which techniques am I going to use to try to stay in the sweet spot?

WE

- As a class, if we were kind and considerate to people, we would benefit and so would they. So much of the worry we all have in our heads would reduce if we got this right. Can we make some changes so that we all feel more connected?

- As a class, discuss this question and write down your suggestions:

  If we all behaved in a pro-social way, and were other-centred and not self-centred, what would we:

  1. stop doing?   2. start doing?   3. continue doing?

- Now turn what you have discussed into a class pledge of five statements. Agree to live by them for two weeks and see what difference it makes. Make sure your teacher puts a reminder in the diary for two weeks' time to discuss what difference it has made to you and to the class.

Chapter 13
Charming

Have you ever been fooled by someone who was very charming? Perhaps they flattered you or were especially kind to you and you enjoyed the attention, only to find out that it was fake, and they were not very kind at all? Or perhaps the opposite is true: that you met someone in the public eye who was very charming and genuine, far more than you had thought they would be? Whatever your experience so far, it is important to be able to spot the genuine from the fake and not to be taken in by charming behaviour.

You may not know it, but it is very likely that you have been brought up with an understanding of the dangers of charm already. There are some very famous Disney characters who show us the problem of charm. How many of these do you know?

- **Gaston from *Beauty and the Beast*:** He starts off charming and over-confident, trying to attract all the ladies of the town, but ends up as a villain obsessed with destroying the Beast. He uses his charm to galvanise the crowd to act hatefully.

- **The Evil Queen from *Snow White*:** The name is a bit of a plot-spoiler here, but she initially appears kind. Underneath it is an obsession with her desire to be the 'fairest of them all' and to remove all competition, including her stepdaughter, Snow White. She uses her charm to lull Snow White (and her father) into a false sense of security before she strikes.

- **Scar from *The Lion King*:** Scar looks like he is the uncle who can offer Simba freedom and some excitement that his parents won't let him have, but it turns out that Scar is obsessed with power and control. He uses his charm to trick the young and innocent Simba and to lead him astray into danger.

Have a think: Which other film characters can you think of who start off looking charming but end up causing complete chaos and destruction? What are they trying to achieve by being charming?

In the last chapter, we explored the idea of *nuance*, where we have to explore different ideas and not just jump to 'yes' or 'no' or 'wrong' or 'right'. Charm is another one of those topics that requires nuance.

Let's define what *charm* means. The word *charm* has meant slightly different things to different people over the years. The word started out referring to a 'magic charm' or a 'song' or 'enchantment', but then became something different. From the 15th to the 17th centuries, it started to mean 'to win over by treating pleasingly' or 'to delight', and then 'a pleasing quality' and 'irresistible power to please and attract'. Today, we have a phrase we use when people are trying to impress us: 'the charm offensive'.

What does charm DO?

Charm does three main things. We will focus on the negative aspects of charm first (but there are many great things about charm that we will come to soon!)

1. **Charm can be used to persuade and convince people.** Public figures usually use charm at some point because they want people to vote for them, or buy their product or to like them. For some, their charm is genuine; they listen, they have integrity, they mean what they say, they present the facts – even if they aren't what people want to hear – and they are kind, considerate people who have a 'presence' about them that is real. Perhaps they have charisma or they focus on making the people in the room feel great. The problem happens when we are persuaded by their charm or charisma. Generally, we like people who are charming and charismatic, and we are very quick to believe what they are saying because of how they are saying it. We might like them and so we are more likely to want to be persuaded by what they are saying.

2. **Charm can be used to manipulate people.** One of the popular sayings about charm is 'deception and seduction walk hand in hand'. What this means is that we are so caught up in our feeling for the person that we can be easily deceived. Let's take Prince Hans and Anna from Disney's *Frozen* as an example. Anna wants to meet someone who she can love and marry; having been isolated in the castle for so long, she is desperate for some attention. The gates are opened for a grand ball

and in walks Prince Hans. Prince Hans is charming and charismatic and sees how desperate Anna is for attention, so he gives her all his attention, and she is so charmed by him that she does all kinds of crazy things, including getting engaged to someone she has just met. Anna is convinced by all he has said, but she has been manipulated by him too. Prince Hans has no intention of ever marrying Anna; he has pretended to fall in love with her so that he can get her power and rule over Arendelle. Sadly, this isn't something that happens only in films.

There are cases all over the world where individuals have fallen for someone's charm and believed they were telling the truth, only to find out they didn't mean any of it. One of the most popular ways that charmers charm is using the 'I am just like you; we are the same' technique. We see this in people who pretend online to be someone they are not, and in famous people who try hard to look 'normal and just like us', despite their great wealth.

3. **Charm can be used as a distraction technique.** We are so easily drawn in by people's charisma and charm that we get distracted from other things they may be doing that may not be quite as charming. It may be that we follow a celebrity who talks eloquently about how much they love us, that they are so grateful for our support and that we can make the world a better place together. We are so taken by this in the moment that we may totally overlook that there have been numerous complaints by their staff about how awfully the celebrity treats them.

Anna, Simba, Snow White and the villagers in *Beauty and the Beast* are all taken in by someone being charming, only to find out that they were persuaded of things that are not true and manipulated because they were distracted by charm.

But I don't want you to think that charm itself is a bad thing; it is not. In fact, charm, when it is real, can be one of the most wonderful things.

People who have a genuine and **natural charm** have the following attributes:

- They are honest; they are not play-acting; they are genuine.
- They are more focused on their inner qualities than their outside appearance.
- They are not asking for anything in return.
- They focus on making people feel connected.
- They help align people to be part of something that helps contribute towards the greater good.
- They help benefit more people than just them; they often benefit a cause.
- They serve others and not just themselves.
- They add, not diminish.
- They make us feel great and empowered.
- They listen.
- They are humble.

Charm is something we often feel in the presence of others; it is a bit elusive. When we know someone who is charming in all the ways that are described above, it can feel wonderful, but it is also real.

Popular movies are full of people who have natural charm: Belle, Kamala Khan (Ms Marvel), Mulan, Cinderella, Rapunzel, Mirabel, Buzz Lightyear, Kristoff, Captain America (both Steve Rogers and Sam Wilson), Shang-Chi and Superman.

Have a think: Who else, real or imagined, do you know who fits the natural-charm criteria?

Charm can be used for great things as well as bad

Let's look at the same three things from earlier, with a little positive twist.

1. **Charm can be used to persuade and convince people.** There are lots of examples of people who have natural charm and use it to make a compelling case for change, and then that change has happened. It might be asking people to fight against poverty or raising money for a cause or asking for people to change their behaviour – we know it works.

2. **Charm can compel people to action.** It doesn't have to manipulate; it can galvanise. When people are galvanised, they are ready to act and DO something. If we see other people really doing what they say they are doing, then we can be inspired to help too. When we see that other people benefit from what they are doing – not just themselves – we may be keener to join in.

3. **Charm can reach places other things cannot reach.** Sometimes meeting someone who has natural charm can make us feel seen, heard, valued and understood. It can help us feel better about ourselves and our circumstances and can give us the pick-me-up that we sometimes need. We don't need to view everyone who is charming with suspicion, but we should check that their behaviour reflects the list under 'natural charm' above.

In his book *Charm: The Elusive Enchantment*, Joseph Epstein sums up the issue of charm brilliantly when he writes:

> Charm will not feed the hungry, end wars, fight evil, yet I happen to believe that the lives of almost all of us are the better for encountering charm. ... It provides a form of necessary relief – relief from the doldrums and the drab everydayness of life. Charm widens the lens, heightens the colour of life, intensifies and sweetens it. We can, of course, all live without it. What a great pity, though, to do so.

Change your world

ME

- How easily persuaded are you by charming people? Have you ever been taken in because someone seemed very convincing but ended up being manipulative or not what you thought they were?

- How charming are you? Being charming can be a great thing if it comes from the right motivation and character. Some things that people may think are 'charming' are just good manners. How many of these things could you do this week? Copy the table and tick them off as you do them!

Number	Natural charm behaviour	Done?
1.	Open doors for people.	
2.	Say 'good morning' or 'hi' as you pass teachers in school.	
3.	Offer to help someone you live with (without asking for any pocket money or something else in return!).	
4.	Write a letter or postcard to a relative you don't see often.	
5.	Say 'thank you' to someone who has done something nice for you this week. (It may be something that they do all the time that you don't usually notice, like the washing-up, washing your clothes or making your tea.)	

- After you have done these things, observe what the reaction is. Have you managed to spread some 'magic' by using your natural charm?

WE

- Unfortunately, in our society, people sometimes use charm to cause harm. As a class, think about what you have already been taught in school about the following situations:

  1. If a stranger approaches you and asks you to go with them.

  2. If someone you don't know befriends you online.

  3. If someone offers you something that sounds too good to be true.

  4. If someone persuades you to do something dangerous or illegal by promising belongings, money or status.

- How can we make sure we do not fall for the 'charm offensive'? What can we do?

Chapter 14
Glow up

Have you ever bought a hair, face or body product because you have seen it advertised on TV, social media or in a shop? Or decided to change the kinds of things you're wearing because a new brand has become popular and is selling out? If you haven't, then someone you know will have done. The 'glow-up' industry is taking the world by storm. What is it and why is it so popular?

The figures for the global beauty industry are staggering. In 2026, it is expected to be worth $703 billion (£526 billion). At a time when people may have found the cost of living a challenge to afford, the beauty industry doesn't seem to have suffered. Here are some interesting facts you may not know!

Did you know?

FACT 1: There is something called the 'lipstick effect', where commentators believe that, in tough financial times, people still like to indulge in the small luxuries that make them feel good. Small items, such as lipstick, can make people feel like they are still having something nice. It doesn't have to be lipstick we're buying of course!

FACT 2: According to Barclays, Gen Z men are the ones who say they spend more of their income on beauty. Men in London spend the most, followed by the East Midlands and Scotland.

FACT 3: Barclays' data also shows that, over the last five years, men's spending on pharmacy, health and beauty categories has increased by 58.1%, which is higher than the figures for women, which are 45.7% for the same period.

FACT 4: According to a management-consulting firm who look at trends and predictions, by 2028 the beauty sector will have a global value of $590 billion (£440 billion) and be growing by 6% each year. It isn't just beauty, but also wellness, that people are taking more seriously.

FACT 5: The industry has also created a whole new dictionary too, with phrases such as 'glow up' and 'contouring' becoming popular, and 'top note', 'heart note' and 'base note' now used to describe how long your aftershave, perfume or body spray stays on!

What's a glow up?!

A 'glow up' is the new slang term for a positive personal transformation. This can mean noticeable changes in someone's appearance or style, but has also been expanded to mean a growth in maturity and confidence. A 'glow up' might happen when you realise what kind of clothes you really want to wear or how confident you look because you are really happy with what you are wearing. All of us have lots of awkward moments when we don't feel like we look our best, but we also have moments when we find our groove and feel more confident.

There is nothing wrong with feeling good because we look good. There is also nothing wrong with taking pride in our appearance and wanting to feel confident because of the work we have done to our outside appearance. Sometimes when we feel we look good, we feel more confident inside. You may have heard the phrase 'fake it till you make it'. That phrase means that we don't always FEEL like we are confident, but sometimes if we act like we are (through making certain clothing choices, for example) our emotions catch up with how we look!

BUT... as you will know by now, this book isn't about the 'glow up' on the outside, however good that can be. It is really about the 'glow up' on the inside: perhaps the most important glow up of all.

Glow up on the inside

In the beauty industry, there are step-by-step guides for pretty much everything: how to apply this, or make your hair do that, but what about our insides? Our hearts and our minds need looking after every bit as much as our faces and bodies, perhaps even more.

There are studies that suggest that an internal change can lead to a 'glow up' externally too. Why? Because how beautiful someone thinks we are is linked to how we behave, how we make them feel and to our character. While initial attraction can be sparked by physical appearance, the research suggests that it is our good character that can deepen our perceived 'beauty'. It also works the other way, though: we may be seen to be attractive on the outside but, if we have negative character traits on the inside, studies show that it impacts how attractive people think we are.

Some alternative beauty facts!

These are some of the findings from research on the impact of someone's character and attitude on their perceived beauty.

1. **Honesty makes us more beautiful.** One study showed that the phrase 'what is good is beautiful' is right. People in the study were asked to rate the attractiveness of lots of people. They were then given a personality description of those people. Then they had to look at their attractiveness rating again. The people who had been described as honest were given higher attractiveness scores by the participants. This is known as the 'honesty premium', and was found to increase the level of attractiveness in the people in the study, regardless of their starting attractiveness score. This 'honesty premium' effect occurred regardless of how attractive the person's clothes were!

2. **Kindness is attractive.** Some studies have shown that kindness, warmth of personality and generosity are seen as more attractive than intelligence or a sense of humour. When people were consistently kind, this was even more effective in attractiveness scores. This is sometimes known as the 'halo effect'. The opposite is also true; those who showed rudeness, lack of kindness and empathy were seen as less attractive to the observers in the study.

3. **Familiarity can help us 'glow up'.** Beauty fades; character deepens. This is known as the 'familiarity effect' because knowing someone can make them more attractive over time. The more comfortable you feel and the more you deepen your understanding of them and they of you, the more you might change your view based on physical appearance alone. Instead of obsessing over only what we wear or what we look like, perhaps we should obsess just as much over talking to people, listening to them, getting to know them and sharing interests and values.

These things work in all relationships, whether friendship or romantic ones. If our inner qualities can change the way people view our physical ones, perhaps we should be spending a lot more time working on our insides?

Have a think: How much work have you done on your insides so that you can become the kind of person who connects to others and be a person who people want to connect with?

Taking care of our appearance and paying attention to what we are wearing is not a bad thing, but those things alone are not what will make people like us and bring us successful, long-lasting relationships. The thing that will draw people to us, and keep connection, is who we are.

We can have a double glow up: inside AND outside.

Change your world

ME

- As we know from Chapter 13, charm needs to be genuine and not manipulative. It takes practice for good characteristics to become a habit, so start working on them now until they ARE who you are. 'Fake it until you make it' works here too. Behave as someone who is kind and you will eventually be kind for yourself.

- Have a look at the list of things that increase attractiveness on the inside. Copy the table. Which ones do you want to work on?

Number	Characteristic	What actions could I do to become these things?
1.	Being kind	
2.	Being generous	
3.	Listening to others	
4.	Spending time with people	
5.	Being honest (telling the truth)	
6.	Laughing with people	
7.	Complimenting others	
8.	Sharing hobbies	
9.	Having a positive attitude	
10.	Showing empathy / compassion	

WE

As a class, vote for which one of the characteristics in the table you want to work on all week individually, but agreed on as a class. For example, you might opt for kindness. Agree together the following things before you start your secret mission:

1. How could you be kind?
2. Who are you going to be kind to? (It could be the lunch staff, the cleaning staff, the reception staff or a different year group.)
3. List what kindness may look like to the group you are going to be kind to, for example opening doors, smiling at people, saying 'hello', asking how people are or thanking someone for your lunch or for cleaning up.
4. Each agree a kindness action that you will do all week. You may even want to keep a record in your planner so you don't forget what impact you had. For example, count the number of people who smile back at you when you have smiled first!
5. Come back at the end of the week and discuss what happened!
   - Has anyone told your teacher how lovely you have been?
   - Has anyone behaved differently back to you?
   - How did you feel doing this secret mission?

Chapter 15
Final thoughts

So what? Lessons for life

We have been through so many topics together, and now we have reached the end. You have considered how you can change and be changed and you have also thought about how we can create change together.

The key to it all is connection: being connected to what we think and feel and being connected to others. It doesn't have to be a choice between 'me' and 'we'; it can, and must, be both. When we think about both *me* and *we*, we are more likely to be happy, fulfilled and healthy and live in communities that are the same too.

I know we have covered a lot. While I know you can reread any of this whenever you want to come back to it, I thought it would be helpful to summarise all the lessons we have covered into one big chart that you can refer to as you move on into the rest of your life.

We started this book together talking about connecting to both 'me' and 'we'. If you keep this list in mind, work on it and try to live by it, it will make a difference, not just to you, but to others too.

How to live CONNECTED through me and we

Number	Living connected
1.	Be brave and tell people you like hanging out with them.
2.	Know that people like you more than you think!
3.	Speak to people in person, not just on social media, so you form real friendships face to face.
4.	If you want a friend, be a friend.
5.	Compare yourself to others if it helps you make sense of yourself.
6.	Compare yourself to others to reveal where you can contribute and add something.
7.	Compare yourself to others to help you be grateful and get perspective.
8.	Compare yourself to others to inspire your own dreams.
9.	Avoid torturing yourself with unhelpful comparison-itus.
10.	When there's a disagreement, think like a scientist – get the facts.
11.	In disagreements, pause to get control of yourself.
12.	In disagreements, own your own feelings, and use 'I' not 'you'.
13.	Be clear about what you want to say, and say it calmly.
14.	Take part in positive or neutral gossip, not negative gossip.
15.	When things get destructive, remove yourself from that conversation.
16.	Make the space and time to really listen to other people.
17.	Ask great questions so people feel your interest.
18.	Focus on letting people shine in the light of your attention; don't steal the spotlight!
19.	Find people like you who you can benefit and encourage.
20.	Find people who are not like you and find something you have in common, however small.
21.	When apologising, know what you are apologising for, take responsibility and ask to put it right.
22.	When someone apologises, thank them and move back to normal.*
23.	Control your brain by allowing some time travel.
24.	Talk to yourself in the second person to bring yourself back under control.
25.	Think in ink to help process your thoughts.
26.	Get outside as often as possible to get perspective.
27.	Find moments of laughter with others.

Number	Living connected
28.	Tell stories to others and bring you and them joy.
29.	Be optimistic by asking, is this permanent, pervasive and / or personal?
30.	Become your own cheerleader.
31.	Cheer on others and help them see the positive.
32.	Decide what you can control and do that.
33.	When you know what needs to change, make a plan of action.
34.	Create good habits by making them obvious, attractive, easy and satisfying.
35.	Break bad habits by making them invisible, unattractive, difficult and unsatisfying.
36.	Decide when you will care what people think and why.
37.	Find the sweet spot between caring too much and too little and try to stay there.
38.	Pay attention to what you think about yourself – be kind to yourself.
39.	Pay attention to what you are paying attention to.
40.	Watch out for people who use charm but have totally selfish motives and may not be all they seem.
41.	Use natural charm to compel people to take action, to motivate and to encourage good.
42.	Focus on your insides as much as your outsides; beauty is more than your face or clothes.
43.	Be consistently honest and kind.
44.	Spend time with people and get to know more than their appearance.
45.	Compliment people and smile at them.
46.	Know that you have more choice than you may think you do.
47.	Always believe in the power you have to change yourself and to help change others too.

*Sometimes there are circumstances when someone does something to you that an apology won't easily fix and a return to normal is not possible or desirable because it is not safe or it is damaging to you in some way. You have adults you can trust at school: if you need to talk to them, do. There are people who can help you if this is the case for you.

'Getting to know you' activities

If we want to feel connected, we have to try to make connections. These simple activities will help you start to build connections with the people you know. They are easy, quick and totally free!

Connecting with other people your own age

Try asking these questions to someone you don't know very well. You might find out you have more in common than you think!

1. Given the choice of anyone in the world, who would you want to chat to for a morning?
2. Would you like to be famous?
3. What is your 'perfect' day?
4. Set a timer for 2 minutes and try and tell your life story.
5. If you could wake up tomorrow and you could have any quality or ability you don't already have, what would it be?
6. What is the best toy you had as a small child?

Connecting with adults in your life

1. If you could wish one thing for me, what would it be?
2. What is your best childhood memory?
3. What toy did you want as a child but were not allowed to have?
4. What is your favourite season and why?

Connecting and laughing through bizarre conversation topics

1. Which body part is the most useful: your nose or your ears?
2. Would you rather stay in a nice hotel that has horrible food or a horrible hotel that has amazing food?

3. Which magical power would you find most useful: being able to be invisible or being able to fly?

4. If you had that magical power, what is the first thing you would do when you had it?

Other activities you could try to build connection

- **Two Truths and a Lie:** Each person shares three statements about themselves, and the group guesses which one is false.

- **Human Bingo:** Create bingo cards of traits, such as 'has a pet', 'plays an instrument' and 'has been to another country'. Students mingle to find classmates who match each square on their bingo card.

- **Speed Friending:** Set up pairs to chat with conversation prompts for 2 to 3 minutes, then rotate.

- **Desert Island:** Students share what three items they'd bring to a desert island and why.

- **Common Ground:** In small groups, students find things they all have in common, beyond the obvious (such as being in the same school). They present their most interesting common find.

- **Emoji Introduction:** Students choose three to five emojis that represent them, and explain their choices.

- **Learn a Dance:** When we are physically in sync with each other, it helps make us feel connected.

- **A Class Playlist:** Agree what your class stands for, and then find your class anthems and create the class playlist.

Getting further support

If you would like to stay connected with other people and volunteer to help others, www.youthemployment.org.uk explains how you can find great opportunities to get involved in helping others.

You don't have to look very far though; here are some things you could do at school:

- Set up a club after school or at lunchtime.

- Find people with similar interests and decide how you can use them to help at school.

- Consider doing an assembly on an issue that you care about.

- Try to raise some money by doing a sponsored event.

- Ask your teacher whether you can write letters to the local elderly care home or visit the residents there at Christmas.

- Offer to tidy up the school grounds.

- Write a letter to your local MP about a local issue you care about.

- Offer to help younger students who need some more support.

There are lots of places to go where you can get free support and help. All these services are recommended via the NHS in the UK. You can find out more, including finding all the links, at www.nhs.uk:

- If you want to read about issues that impact young people, visit: www. youngminds.org.uk. There are videos by topic and lots of things for you to read and listen to, but also lots of support for your parents too.

- If you need someone to speak to for counselling or online support, ChildLine provides a confidential telephone and online counselling service for anyone under 19. You can call 0800 1111 any time for free – lines are open 24 hours a day – or have an online chat with a Childline counsellor: www.childline.org.uk

- The Mix (www.themix.org.uk) provides a free confidential telephone helpline and online service for anyone under 25. It aims to find young people the best help, whatever the problem. You can call 0808 808 4994 for free – lines are open from 11am to 11pm every day.

If you feel like you are in crisis and need urgent help:

- The Samaritans (www.samaritans.org) are an organisation you can ring at any time of the day or night. They'll help you and listen to how you're feeling. You can call them free and confidentially on 116 123 – lines are open 24 hours a day – or email them at jo@samaritans.org

- SHOUT (www.giveusashout.org) provides free, confidential, 24/7 text-message support in the UK for anyone who is struggling to cope and anyone in crisis. You can text SHOUT to 85258.

References

Chapter 1

Statistics on loneliness in America:

Harvard Graduate School of Education, 'What is Causing Our Epidemic of Loneliness and How Can We Fix It?' [online] Available at: www.gse. harvard.edu/ideas/usable-knowledge/24/10/what-causing-our-epidemic-loneliness-and-how-can-we-fix-it Accessed: 27 August 2025.

How steep a hill appears:

Schnall, S. (2008) 'Social Support and the Perception of Geographical Slant', *National Library of Medicine* [online] Available at: https://pmc.ncbi. nlm.nih.gov/articles/PMC3291107 Accessed: 27 August 2025.

Connection linked to health:

World Health Organization, 'Social connection linked to improved health and reduced risk of early death' [online] Available at: www.who.int/news/ item/30-06-2025-social-connection-linked-to-improved-heath-and-reduced-risk-of-early-death Accessed: 27 August 2025.

World Health Organization, 'From loneliness to social connection: charting a path to healthier societies' [online] Available at: www.who.int/groups/ commission-on-social-connection/report Accessed: 27 August 2025.

Fact 4:

Robson, D. (2025) *The Laws of Connection*. Edinburgh: Canongate Books, p.2.

Cambridge Dictionary, 'epidemic' [online] Available at: https://dictionary. cambridge.org/dictionary/english/epidemic Accessed: 27 August 2025.

Brown, B. 'The Power of Vulnerability' TEDTalk, *YouTube* [online] Available at: www.youtube.com/watch?v=iCvmsMzlF7o Accessed: 15 February 2026, quotation 'Connection is why we're here. It's what gives purpose and meaning to our lives. This is what it's all about.' (3 minutes 20).

Chapter 2

Kross, E. (2026) *Shift: How to Manage Your Emotions So They Don't Manage You.* London: Vermilion, p.156.

Facts on influencers:

Digital Marketing Institute, '20 Surprising Influencer Marketing Statistics' [online] Available at: https://digitalmarketinginstitute.com/blog/20-influencer-marketing-statistics-that-will-surprise-you Accessed: 7 February 2026.

Sinek, S. (2020) *The Infinite Game.* London: Portfolio Penguin.

Forbes (2026) 'Taylor Swift' [online] Available at: www.forbes.com/profile/taylor-swift Accessed: 15 February 2026.

Chapter 3

Grant, A. (2022) "You can't say that!': how to argue, better', *The Guardian* [online] Available at: www.theguardian.com/lifeandstyle/2022/jul/30/you-cant-say-that-how-to-argue-better Accessed: 5 September 2025.

Scott, S. (2017) *Fierce Conversations: Achieving Success at Work & in Life, One Conversation at a Time.* London: Piatkus.

Robinson, B.E. PhD (2020) 'The 90-Second Rule That Builds Self-Control' in *Psychology Today* [online] Available at: www.psychologytoday.com/gb/blog/the-right-mindset/202004/the-90-second-rule-builds-self-control Accessed: 23 September 2025.

Chapter 4

Workspace, 'Workplace gossip – turning back the tide' [online] Available at: www.workspace.co.uk/content-hub/business-insight/workplace-gossip-turning-back-the-tide#:~:text=If%20you've%20ever%20worked,originate%20from%20a%20harmful%20place Accessed: 15 February 2026.

Stade, L. 'Gossip at School: Who spreads rumours and how do we stop them?', *Linda Stade Education* [online] Available at: https://lindastade.com/gossip-at-school/#:~:text=However%2C%20gossip%20can%20be%20broken,75%25%20of%20gossip%20is%20neutral Accessed: 7 February 2026.

University of Michigan, 'Boys gossip just as much as girls, study shows' [online] Available at: https://news.umich.edu/boys-gossip-just-as-much-as-girls-study-shows Accessed: 7 February 2026.

Gottfried, S. (2019) 'The Science Behind Why People Gossip – And When It Can Be a Good Thing', *Time* [online] Available at: https://time.com/5680457/why-do-people-gossip Accessed 7 February 2026.

Association for Psychological Science (2019) 'We Gossip About 52 Minutes A Day. That May Not Be As Toxic As It Sounds' [online] Available at: www.psychologicalscience.org/news/we-gossip-about-52-minutes-a-day-that-may-not-be-as-toxic-as-it-sounds.html#:~:text=Almost%20everyone%20gossips.,nor%20negative%2C"%20Robbins%20says Accessed: 15 February 2026.

Dunbar, R. (2020) *Grooming, Gossip and the Evolution of Language*. Cambridge, Massachusetts: Harvard University Press.

Anwar, Y. (2012) 'Gossip isn't all bad — new study finds its social and psychological benefits', *UC Berkeley* [online] Available at: https://news.berkeley.edu/2012/01/17/gossip/#:~:text=Observers'%20heart%20rates%20increased%20as,to%20engage%20in%20the%20gossip Accessed: 15 February 2026.

Warren, J.D. (2019) 'Study busts myths about gossip', *University of California* [online] Available at: www.universityofcalifornia.edu/news/study-busts-myths-about-gossip#:~:text=Younger%20people%20engage%20in%20more,all%20three%20types%20of%20gossip Accessed: 15 February 2026.

Chapter 5

Murphy, K. (2020) *You're Not Listening: What You're Missing and Why It Matters*. London: Harvill Secker.

Chapter 6

The Decision Lab, 'The Similar-To-Me Effect' [online] Available at: https://thedecisionlab.com/reference-guide/psychology/the-similar-to-me-effect Accessed 7 February 2026.

Voss, C. (2017) *Never Split the Difference: Negotiating as if your life depended on it*. New York: Random House Business.

Chapter 7

Robbins, R. 'The art of the mindful apology' [online] Available at: www.tonyrobbins.com/blog/mindful-apology?srsltid=AfmBOoq01vGd3dFXCAYpCfLKG3_HI11af6VdM7gD1Wm9pq8wllWCq2dM Accessed: 8 February 2026.

Grabmeier, J. (2016) 'The 6 elements of an effective apology, according to science', *Ohio State News* [online] Available at: https://news.osu.edu/the-6-elements-of-an-effective-apology-according-to-science Accessed: 15 February 2026.

Chapter 8

Kershner. A. (2023) 'The Fast and the Frustrated: Why Our Speedy Brains Make It Harder To Pay Attention & Listen Effectively', *Medium* [online] Available at: https://medium.com/@alikershner/the-fast-and-the-frustrated-why-our-speedy-brains-make-it-harder-to-pay-attention-listen-d217814b15e0 Accessed: 8 February 2026.

Kross, E. (2022) *Chatter*. London: Vermilion.

Tversky, B. (2019) 'To understand how people think, look to their actions, not their words, Stanford scholar says', *Stanford University* [online] Available at: https://news.stanford.edu/stories/2019/08/thinking-faster-words Accessed: 16 October 2025.

Barnard, D. (2022) 'Average Speaking Rate and Words per Minute', *Virtual Speech* [online] Available at: https://virtualspeech.com/blog/average-speaking-rate-words-per-minute Accessed: 16 October 2025.

Suddendorf, T. and Corballis, M.C. (2007) 'The evolution of foresight: What is mental time travel, and is it unique to humans?', *National Library of Medicine* [online] Available at: https://pubmed.ncbi.nlm.nih.gov/17963565 Accessed: 16 October 2025.

'Humans The Only Species Capable of Mental Time Travel: Study', *NDTV World* (2015) [online] Available at: www.ndtv.com/world-news/humans-the-only-species-capable-of-mental-time-travel-study-1258214 Accessed: 16 October 2025.

Chapter 9

Gerloff, P. (2011) 'You're Not Laughing Enough, and That's No Joke', *Psychology Today* [online] Available at: www.psychologytoday.com/gb/blog/the-possibility-paradigm/201106/youre-not-laughing-enough-and-thats-no-joke Accessed: 8 February 2026.

Heggie, B.-A. (2019) 'The Healing Power of Laughter', *National Library of Medicine* [online] Available at: https://pmc.ncbi.nlm.nih.gov/articles/PMC6609137 Accessed: 8 February 2026.

Suttie, J. (2017) 'How Laughter Brings Us Together', *Greater Good Magazine* [online] Available at: https://greatergood.berkeley.edu/article/item/how_laughter_brings_us_together Accessed: 8 February 2026.

Scott, S. (2019) 'I'm a scientist studying laughter – and it's funnier than you might think', *The Guardian* [online] Available at: www.theguardian.com/commentisfree/2019/apr/15/scientist-studying-laughter-funny-comedy Accessed: 8 February 2026.

Kaercher Kramer, C. and Bauermann Leitao, C. (2023) 'Laughter as medicine: A systematic review and meta-analysis of interventional studies evaluating the impact of spontaneous laughter on cortisol levels', *National Library of Medicine* [online] Available at: https://pmc.ncbi.nlm.nih.gov/articles/PMC10204943 Accessed: 8 February 2026.

Gonot-Schoupinsky, F. (2021) 'How to laugh more', *Psyche* [online] Available at: https://psyche.co/guides/how-to-get-a-health-and-wellbeing-boost-from-laughing Accessed: 8 February 2026.

Berger, A.A. (2017) *The Art of Comedy Writing*. London: Routledge.

Chapter 10

Oxford English Dictionary [online] Available at: www.oed.com Accessed: 8 February 2026.

Hood, B. (2024) 'Optimism and health', *The Psychologist* [online] Available at: www.bps.org.uk/psychologist/optimism-and-health Accessed: 8 February 2026.

Scott, E. PhD (2026) 'What Does It Mean to Be an Optimist?', *verywellmind* [online] Available at: www.verywellmind.com/the-benefits-of-optimism-3144811 Accessed: 8 February 2026.

Houston, E. BSc (2019) 'The Theory of Explanatory Styles', *Positive Psychology* [online] Available at: https://positivepsychology.com/explanatory-styles-optimism/#the-theory-of-explanatory-styles Accessed: 8 February 2026.

Chapter 11

'How Social Media Keeps You Hooked – An expose on how the apps we use every day are designed to grab and hold your attention', *Freedom* (2023) [online] Available at: https://freedom.to/blog/how-social-media-keeps-you-hooked/#:~:text=According%20to%20Psychologist%20Nir%20Eyal,Action Accessed: 8 February 2026.

'Understanding the Psychology behind Social Media Addiction: How Platforms Use the Hooked Framework for Habit Formation', *Medium* (2023) [online] Available at: https://medium.com/design-bootcamp/understanding-the-psychology-behind-social-media-addiction-how-platforms-use-the-hooked-framework-c25f1ba41c79 Accessed: 8 February 2026.

Clear, J. [online] Available at: https://jamesclear.com Accessed: 8 February 2026.

Easthope, L. (2025) *Come What May*. London: Hodder Press.

Chapter 12

Chamorro-Premuzic, T. (2025) *Don't Be Yourself: Why Authenticity Is Overrated (and What to Do Instead)*. Massachusetts: Harvard Business Review Press.

Becker-Phelps, L. PhD (2023) 'Why You Care What Others Think, and Why It's Not a Bad Thing', *Psychology Today* [online] Available at: www.psychologytoday.com/gb/blog/making-change/202308/why-you-care-what-others-think-and-why-its-not-a-bad-thing Accessed: 8 February 2026.

Raghunathan, R. PhD (2016) 'How Not to Worry About What Others Think of You', *Psychology Today* [online] Available at: www.psychologytoday.com/gb/blog/sapient-nature/201603/how-not-worry-about-what-others-think-you Accessed: 8 February 2026.

Susan Dominus, S. (2013) 'Is Giving the Secret to Getting Ahead?', *The New York Times Magazine* [online] Available at: www.nytimes.

com/2013/03/31/magazine/is-giving-the-secret-to-getting-ahead.html#
Accessed: 8 February 2026.

Reed Turrell, E. (2021) *Please Yourself.* London: 4th Estate.

Catmull, E. (2014) *Creativity, Inc.: Overcoming the Unseen Forces That Stand in the Way of True Inspiration.* London: Random House.

Grant, A. (2016) *Originals: How Non-Conformists Move the World.* New York: Viking.

Chapter 13

Epstein, J. (2018) *Charm: The Elusive Enchantment.* Lyons Press: Connecticut.

Etymonline [online] Available at: www.etymonline.com/word/charm Accessed: 15 February 2026.

Chapter 14

Statista, 'Beauty & Personal Care – Worldwide' [online] Available at: www.statista.com/outlook/cmo/beauty-personal-care/worldwide#revenue Accessed: 15 February 2026.

McKinsey & Company (2024) 'The beauty boom and beyond: Can the industry maintain its growth?' [online] Available at: www.mckinsey.com/industries/consumer-packaged-goods/our-insights/the-beauty-boom-and-beyond-can-the-industry-maintain-its-growth   Accessed: 15 February 2026.

Gulati, A. et al., (2024) 'What is beautiful is still good: the attractiveness halo effect in the era of beauty filters', *National Library of Medicine* [online] Available   at: https://pmc.ncbi.nlm.nih.gov/articles/PMC11597472 Accessed: 8 February 2026.

Cherry, K. MSEd (2025) 'The Halo Effect in Psychology', *VeryWellMind* [online] Available at: www.verywellmind.com/what-is-the-halo-effect-2795906#:~:text=the%20product%20itself.-,The%20Reverse%20Halo%20(or%20Horn)%20Effect,Read%20more:&text=Rasmussen%20K.,Publications%2C%20Inc.;%202004 Accessed: 15 February 2026.

Hill, A. (2024) "I can see change spreading": why male grooming is booming', *The Guardian* [online] Available at: www.theguardian.com/fashion/2024/jan/12/i-can-see-change-spreading-why-male-grooming-is-booming Accessed: 8 February 2026.

'Man in the mirror: How male beauty spending is reshaping the industry', *Barclays* [online] Available at: https://home.barclays/insights/2025/06/male-beauty-spending/#:~:text=Growth%20in%20men's%20beauty%20spending,increase%20for%20women%20(5.8%25) Accessed: 8 February 2026.

'The Complete Guide To Men's Grooming Jargon', *FashionBeans* (2025) [online] Available at: www.fashionbeans.com/article/mens-grooming-jargon Accessed: 8 February 2026.

Niimi, R. and Goto, M. (2023) 'Good conduct makes your face attractive: The effect of personality perception on facial attractiveness judgments', *National Library of Medicine* [online] Available at: https://pmc.ncbi.nlm.nih.gov/articles/PMC9925008/#:~:text=Indeed%2C%20some%20studies%20showed%20that,at%20all%20or%20only%20slightly Accessed: 8 February 2026.

Alania, M. (2023) 'The Science of Attraction: Understanding the Psychological Factors That Influence Connections', *Quick and Dirty Tips* [online] Available at: www.quickanddirtytips.com/articles/the-science-of-attraction-understanding-the-psychological-factors-that-influence-connections/#:~:text=Personality%20traits%20play%20a%20significant,repel%20potential%20partners%20or%20friends Accessed: 8 February 2026.

'The psychology of attraction: Why do we fancy certain people?', *BBC Bitesize* [online] Available at: www.bbc.co.uk/bitesize/articles/zm9ry9q#:~:text=proximity:%20how%20near%20you%20are,is%20a%20little%20bit%20weird Accessed: 8 February 2026.

Personalised professional development from Hachette Learning Academy

A simple way to boost career progression, staff motivation and educational excellence.

Our online courses are:

 Aligned with **teaching competency frameworks**

 Written by experts in education, including Hachette Learning authors (formerly John Catt)

 Created to enable educators to **develop competencies** linked to their professional development aspirations

 Powered by adaptive learning, to accommodate a diverse range of skills, knowledge and understanding

 Designed to support **effective learning and high-impact teaching**

www.hachettelearning.com/academy